Samuel Birch

Egypt from the Earliest Times to B.C. 300

Samuel Birch

Egypt from the Earliest Times to B.C. 300

ISBN/EAN: 9783337227418

Printed in Europe, USA, Canada, Australia, Japan

Cover: Foto ©ninafisch / pixelio.de

More available books at **www.hansebooks.com**

ANCIENT HISTORY

FROM THE MONUMENTS.

EGYPT

FROM THE

EARLIEST TIMES TO B. C. 300.

BY

S. BIRCH, LL.D., ETC.

NEW YORK:
SCRIBNER, ARMSTRONG & CO.
1875.

Grant, Faires & Rodgers,
Electrotypers and Printers,
52 & 54 N. Sixth St.
Philadelphia.

CONTENTS.

INTRODUCTION..Page vii.

CHAPTER I.

Old Empire, from the first to the close of the sixth dynasty. From about 3000 B.C. to 2000 B.C. First dynasty—Menes—Athothis—Ousaphais. Second dynasty—Bœthos—Sent—Pyramid of Meydoum. Third dynasty—Monuments at Sakkarah. Fourth dynasty—Cheops—Kephren—Mencheres—Pyramids of Gizeh—Civilization—Manners. Fifth dynasty—Sahura—Mines of the Wady Magarah—Papyrus of Ptahhetp. Sixth dynasty—Pepi—Exploits of Una—Negroes......................................Page 23

CHAPTER II.

Middle Empire, from the seventh to the eighteenth dynasty. From about 2000 B.C. to 1600 B.C. Eleventh dynasty—Antef—Tombs at the El-Assasif—Mentuhetp valley of El Hammamat. Twelfth dynasty—War of Osertesen I.—Famine in Egypt—Ethiopian wars—Supposed arrival of Hebrews—Amenemha III.—Lake Mœris—Temple of the Sarabit-el-Khadim—Amenemha IV.—Labyrinth, lake and pyramids. Thirteenth dynasty—Invasion of the Hyk-shos or Shepherd rulers..................Page 59

CHAPTER III.

New Empire from the eighteenth to the twentieth dynasty. From 1600 B.C. to 1110 B.C. Expulsion of Shepherds—Exploits of Aahmes I.—Thothmes I.—The Queen Hasheps—Arabian tributes and queen—Wars of Thothmes III.—Battle of Megiddo—Tributes—Exploits of Amenemheb—Amenophis III.—Heretical worship of the sun's disk—Restoration of the worship of Amen—Seti I. and his wars—Rameses II.—Great war with the Khita and treaty—Period of the Exodus—Meneptah, supposed Pharaoh—New hypothesis of route—Invasion of Egypt by Libyans, Greeks, and Italians—Rameses III.—War with Libyans, and Pelasgi—His riches and luxury—Rameses XII—Mission of the ark of the god Khons to Bakhlan—Fall of the Ramessids............Page 81

CHAPTER IV.

From the twenty-first dynasty to the conquest. From about 1100 B.C. to 332 B.C.—Family of Shisak—Conquest of Jerusalem—Death of an Apis—Invasion of Piankhi the Ethiopian—Submission of Nimrod—Exploits of Piankhi—Bokchoris—Sabaco—Tirhakah—Conquest of Egypt by Esarhaddon—Invasion of Egypt by Tirhakah—Re-conquest by Assur-bani-pal—Rutamen—Nutmiamen—Psammetichus I.—Gyges—Greek mercenaries—Tombs of the Apis—Apries—Amasis—Conquest of Egypt by Cambyses—Darius—Revolt of Egypt—Xerxes—Artaxerxes—Nechterebes—Teos—Conquest of Egypt by Alexander..Page 162

INTRODUCTION.

ANCIENT Egypt is one of the two great countries of the world which has performed so important a part in the religious history of the East, that its annals, as derived from the monuments, are of the greatest importance to understanding the development of human civilization and the tendency of religious thought. It was in it that the Hebrews passed their first captivity, entering it as a nomad race with their flocks and herds, and leaving the house of bondage with the knowledge and arts of its early civilization. The land itself, called in the hieroglyphics **Kam** or the Black, from the color of the alluvial mud of the Nile, bore several other names in the Egyptian language. To the Hebrews it was known as Mitsraim or the Two Mitsrs, an appellation found also in the Assyrian as Musr, and the Persian as Mudraya, but the Greeks called it Aiguptos, a word of uncertain derivation retained at the present day as Egypt, by which it is universally known. No country could have been better fitted for the cradle of the human race: blessed with a rainless sky, a fertile soil, an incessant supply of water, and protected by its conformation from the disaster of early conquest, it possessed all that was necessary for the happiness and safety of its population. It was the bed of the river Nile, which in a course of miles received no tributary stream into its bosom, but, supplied by the outpour of the great lakes of Central Africa, annually spread its waters over a barren desert, which it fertilized; retiring again to a narrower bed, it left behind it a long and narrow strip of cultivatable land not exceeding the breadth of a few miles till it reached the modern Fayoum or ancient Delta, where the waters of the rivers, mostly repelled by the Mediterranean, threw down in the shape of a fan the mud they carried in their course, as the choked watercourses gradually silted up. Two ranges of low and barren hills, granite at Syene, sandstone a little beyond, and limestone till they reach the Fayoum, skirt the Valley of the Nile, beyond which lies the arid and lifeless desert. It was in this valley, teeming with vegetable and animal life, that the ancient Egyptians flourished and erected those vast edifices, the admiration of all ages.

It is a peculiarity of this country that the absence of rain, the great destroyer of works of art, has enabled even the most fragile materials, such as rapidly perish elsewhere, to survive the slow process of destroying time, for all above the level of the inundation was safe from the usual elements of decay. The inundation took place at the 28th July or about the summer solstice, and almost to a day; the river as it rose changing rapidly in color, especially in Upper Egypt, from a slimy green to a turbid red color. And when it attained a height of sixteen cubits it revived the drooping vegetation of the cultivated lands, which no drop of rain from heaven ever watered except at long and distant intervals of time.

The race of men by whom the Valley of the Nile was tenanted, was considered in their legends to have been created by the gods out of clay; a legend closely resembling the Mosaic account of the creation of man. Modern researches have, however, not as yet finally determined if advancing from Western Asia they entered the alluvial land bringing with them an already developed civilization; or if ascending from Ethiopia they followed the course of the river to its mouth; or if they were Aborigines, the date of whose appearance is beyond the knowledge of man and the scan of science. On the earliest monuments they appear as a red or dusky race, with features neither entirely Caucasian nor Nigritic; more resembling at the earliest age the European, at the middle period of the Empire the Nigritic races or the offspring of a mixed population, and at the most flourishing period of their Empire the sallow tint and refined type of the Semitic families of mankind. Placed in the Mosaic accounts as descendants of the family of Ham, or the Black races, it has been usual to style them Hamitic, as an African people. At all periods of history the development, both physical and intellectual, of the Egyptians was of a high order; offering a marked contrast with the Nigritic nations, whom nothing but the pressure of conquest or subjection can elevate to a higher standard, owing to the early arrest of physical and intellectual growth. It is not to be supposed that Egypt was alone inhabited at the time of its earliest monuments. It had soon come in conflict with adjacent countries already partly populated. South of Syene lay the numerous black tribes, the so-called *Nahsi* or Negroes, inferior in civilization but turbulent and impatient of subjection. The skirts of the Eastern desert were held by wandering tribes called Satu, not yet subjected to the arms and discipline of Egypt. The Western frontier was menaced by the Tahennu or Libyans, but the waters of the Mediterranean had not as yet been infested as at a later period by the Phœnicians and Greeks, who exercised the arts of piracy and commerce. Beyond the North-eastern desert, in which resided the Herusha or Inhabitants of the Waste, were the *Menat*, perhaps also a Shepherd race, the dwellers of Northern Asia; and hazily in the distance were seen the nascent forms of the Empires of Babylon and Assyria, and the slowly rising power of the Phœnician states and Syrian kingdoms.

The religious notions of the Egyptians were chiefly

connected with the worship of the Sun, with whom at a later period all the principal deities were connected. As Har or Harmachis he represented the youthful or rising Sun, as Ra the mid-day, and as Tum the setting Sun. According to Egyptian notions, that god floated in a boat through the sky or celestial ether, and descended to the dark regions of night or Hades. Many deities attended on his passage or were connected with his worship, and the gods Amen and Kheper, who represented the invisible and the self-produced god, were identified with the Sun. The soul was supposed to have emanated from the deity, and after death passed to the great judgment in the Hall of Truth, where it was judged by Osiris, the Egyptian Pluto, and the forty-two daimons or judges of the dead. Hence according to its merits it went into the boat of the Sun, the Elysian fields, the pools of peace, and other abodes of bliss; or else passing through the house of truth, transmigrated or reappeared on earth in some animal or human form suitable to its demerits. The idea of a single self-existent deity was indeed stated in the hymns and prayers addressed to certain gods, who are said to have animated or produced all beings, or to have been the universal and animating principle of nature. In the different sects Ptah was thought to have produced the Sun and Moon, or celestial bodies, Khnum mankind, and Tum or the setting Sun existences and beings. At a later period the eight great gods were considered different in the colleges of Thebes and Memphis. According to the later traditions the gods had reigned over Egypt prior to the native kings, and in the Memphite registers the first of the series was Ptah or Vulcan, the lord of the cubit, the demiurgos of the Kosmos or Universe. He was succeeded by Ra, the meridian or mid-day Sun, Ra by Shu, another form of the same luminary allied with his sister Tef. These were followed by Seb or Saturn, the prince of the gods, and apparently the stellar universe allied to Nut or the Ether, like the Greek Rhea, from whom sprung the terrestrial gods. Osiris, the universal god of Egypt, with his wife Isis succeeded. Then came Set or Typhon, the brother and rival of Osiris, and the evil principle of Egyptian mythology. Lastly came Horus, the conqueror of Set, the avenger of his father, and the immediate predecessor of the demigods. These deities were supposed to have reigned 13,900 years, and to have been succeeded by the followers of Horus, who ruled for 4000 years more. The succession at Thebes followed nearly the same order, but Amon Ra, the Theban Jupiter was placed at the head of the list, although the evidence of the monuments proves that his appearance in the mythology was later than that of Ptah. The god Mentu, another form of the Sun, and who gave his name to the Theban Hermonthis, was substituted for Ra, but the after succession followed the same order, and was closed by the reign of Har or Horus and his wife Hathor or Athor, 'the abode of Horus,' the Egyptian Venus and the lord goddess of Dendera or Tentyris, Athribis, and Aphroditopolis. Besides the gods of the first order, twelve were reckoned in the second order, amongst whom were Tahuti or Thoth, the god of wisdom and knowledge, inventor of speech and writing and the arts and sciences, and the patron of scribes and authors; and Anup or Anubis, son of Osiris, and the director of the funereal rites and embalmer of the dead. There was a third order, but its members are not known, although it comprised some of the numerous deities seen on the monuments, the attendants, ministers, or companions of the principal gods. In the local worship of the great gods, a kind of triad or three principal persons of the family appeared. At Memphis they were Ptah, his wife Merenphtah, and his son Nefer-Atum. A second female goddess Bast, lion-headed like Merenphtah and probably her sister, was also occasionally seen. At Heliopolis the triad consisted of Tum or Harmachis, Nebhetp, and Horus. At Abydos of Osiris, Isis his wife, and Horus, to whom Nephthys was sometimes added; while at Elephantine Khnum or Chnoumis and the goddess Anuka or Anoucis and their son Hak, formed the local triad. Besides these were various other local triads in all the chief cities of the country. The gods were represented with human or animal heads, by which last and the head attire they were distinguished thus from each other. Of the human-headed deities, Amen-Ra wore two plumes of hawks' feathers, a disk, and red cap; Osiris, a conical cap placed on horns and flanked by ostrich feathers; Anhor, Onouris or Mars, four feathers; Ra and the gods of the Sun had hawks' heads; Khnum, that of a ram; Sebak, a crocodile's head; Thoth, the head of an ibis; and Anubis, that of a jackal. The uræus or cobra di capella snake often appeared on their heads, and they held in their hands emblems of life, and sceptres terminating in the head of a mystic animal; goddesses sometimes carried sceptres in shape of the stem of a papyrus.

Attached to the worship were the sacred animals, which were supposed to be incarnations of the efflatus or spirit of the gods. The most remarkable of these were the bull, Hapi or Apis, emblems of the moon and the sacred life of the god Ptah, worshipped at Memphis; Mnevis, another bull sacred to the Sun at Heliopolis; another sacred bull, Pacis, at Hermonthis; and the white cow of Athor at Athribis. These animals dwelt in the adyta of the temples; and all the principal animals of the country had representations of the gods, as apes or cynocephali sacred to the moon in his type of Khons at Thebes, the fish latus at Eileithyia, and the crocodile in the Arsinoite nome. Some of these animals were selected from the rest by particular marks, and all had honors paid them during life, and were carefully embalmed after death.

The Egyptians possessed an extensive literature, the invention of the art of writing being due to them. By means of the hieroglyphs or direct representation of celestial, terrestrial and other objects, they expressed sounds or ideas, and by the union of the two their language. For the ordinary purposes of life a cursive or writing-hand, called the hieratic, consisting of an abridged form of the hieroglyphs was adopted, and by means of this their books were written, in black and red characters, on a thin paper called papyrus, formed out of slices of a reed with a prismatic stem, known as the cyperus. Their books were not divided into pages and bound like modern volumes, but written on long rolls of paper in short pages, by means of a frayed reed. The principal works in the literature were religious, as the Book of the Dead or Ritual, in which are the principal prayers, directions for amulets, descriptions of the Elysium, Hades or hell, and esoterical explanations of the meaning of the ancient symbolism. The Book of the Lamentations or sighs of Isis; hymns to different gods; ethical treatises on morals, and others on rhetoric. In medicine, chiefly of an empirical nature, and much mixed up with charms and adjurations, several treatises ascribed to the oldest dynasties are known; others of geometry, mensuration, and arithmetic, are also extant, while the political and social conditions of Egypt are illustrated by the reports and indictments drawn up by scribes, registers of the donations made to temples, or of things received by the crown or individuals. Nor were works of imagination wanting to while away the leisure or heavier hours of the reading class, and some of them as remote as the twelfth dynasty. History is only represented by one or two lists of kings, and details of public events, but is amply illustrated by the basreliefs and hieroglyphical inscriptions of the principal monuments of the country, in which conquests and other great public events, are described in heroic strains.

In their moral law the Egyptians followed the same precepts as the decalogue, and crimes were punished according to their enormity; the bastinado was administered to obtain confessions, as a punishment for minor offences, while serious crimes were visited with excision of the nose and ears, or death by decapitation. Treason, murder, adultery, theft, and the practice of magic were crimes of the deepest dye, and punished accordingly. In domestic life the Egyptian was attached to his wife and children, and the equality of the female sex with the male most marked; the Egyptian woman appearing always as the equal and companion of her father, brethren, and husband. She was never secluded in a harem like the Asiatic lady, but appeared in private company or public rites, participated in equal rights before the law, served in the priesthood, and even mounted the throne. She was thought to have a soul the same as man, unlike the conceptions of Islam. Her name is mentioned in the genealogies of families. Unfortunately, the women known in Egyptian history or depicted by romance, do not bear a good character, nor is it probable that their education was sedulously conducted, as no literary compositions or other writings of women are known. They form, in this respect, a striking contrast with the remarkable women mentioned in the Scriptures. They, however, were accomplished in music, and some of the other arts and sciences. Both sexes sat at table on chairs or on the ground; and the Egyptian never reclined like the luxurious Assyrian or Greek while his wife sat respectfully on the chair at the foot of the couch. In eating the hands only were used, and the only appliances on the table were the bowls and mats which held the viands. Children under the age of puberty went undressed, princesses not excepted, an African custom; but on attaining that age they wore a peculiar lock of hair at the left side, while youths and men were dressed; men always with a short fluted garment round the loins called shenti or sindon. Persons of high rank wore garments of fine linen reaching to the ankles, and with full sleeves. Females seldom had more than a single garment from the breast to the ankles, relieved by straps across the shoulders. Sandals were not worn till the fifth dynasty, and then not always, and at the time of the twentieth they had long recurved toes. They were made of leather, papyrus, and palm fibres. The priests wore only papyrus. Shoes were unknown. Linen only was used; cotton was unknown. Even armor was of linen; but leather seems to have been employed for some parts of the dress. The hair and beard was often shaved, especially of priests and persons of high class, and the barber in full activity went from street to street. Fashions, however, varied, and the front portion of the beard was left and made into a square shape, or recurved, perhaps, with the addition of ribbons. Both sexes blackened the brows and lids of the eyes with kohl or stibium; cosmetics for the skin, and pastilles for the breath were used, the nails were died with *henna*, and crowns of flowers wound round the hair to augment female beauty. The ornaments worn by both sexes were nearly the same, collars of rows of beads and chains of gold round the neck, armlets and bracelets of gold, inlaid with lapis-lazuli and turquoise round the arms, and anklets of the same round the ankles. Females only wore earrings, but both sexes loaded their fingers with rings, some of which were used as seals or signets. Men of rank and authority often bore a cylindrical stick, sometimes terminating in shape of a papyrus, and on many of these are affectionate addresses to that stay and support of their old age. In ceremonies, peculiar sceptres or batons were used. Mirrors such as the Hebrew women melted to make the tabernacles, razors, tweezers and hair pins were also in use for the the toilet.

The Egyptian sat either on a chair or else on the ground, often on the knees, sometimes with the legs crossed. In prayer he knelt or stood, but always raised both hands with the palms outwards before him. Slaves and inferiors sat to hear the words of their superiors, or even prostrated themselves on the belly before them, and the sandals were taken off when approaching the royal presence. The head was either shorn, covered with a wig or else a close-fitting cap, according to the caste and sex. Great politeness was observed, a spirit of hospitality prevailed, and the scribes often inveighed against the abuse of wine and beer, freely indulged in by youth. For amusements, jugglers, acrobats, and pantomimic dances helped to shorten the weary hours, with the game of draughts or robbers, that of the base played with many pieces, and morra. Women sported at ball, danced, spun, and sewed. The youthful aristocracy indulged in the pleasures of the chase, harpooned the crocodile or hippopotamus, shot, with arrows, gazelles and other game or animals, trapped the hyæna, netted fish or water fowl, and angled in the pond or stream. At an early age the military caste went to barracks and were drilled to Egyptian arms, the bow and arrow, the dagger, lance, mace, and shield, or were instructed in the management of the horse and chariot, although it was usually driven by a groom or coachman. The art of writing was early taught, and the education extended to the circle of Egyptian literature. Elegant furniture adorned the house; chairs and footstools, couches and head-rests, or pillows in shape of a lune upon a stand, with cushions and pillows of feathers of the water-fowl. The public architecture was on the grandest scale, and dwarfs the Greek on comparison. Gigantic columns with lotus or papyrus capitals, towered to a height of sixty feet. Others, the models of the Greek Doric, appear at the early period of the twelfth dynasty, while, at a later time, the lotus capital suggested the Ionic volute. A blaze of colors adorned the architecture and charmed the eye, and picture was its pleasure. In sculpture the hardest materials, the rose granite, the green basalt, as well as the soft limestone, were carved into required shapes, adjusted to a rigid canon. The walls swarmed with colored patterns, devices, and hieroglyphs, miniature portraits of things in heaven, on earth, and under the water. Architecture, sculpture, and painting descended as mourners to the grave. In the dark sepulchral passages where no sunlight enters, the torch reveals careful though unshaded painting, and brilliant colors laid in tempera on the walls by the artist, who must have worked to the gloomy flicker of the lamp. In chambers of the pierced and tunnelled hills, lay the mummies of the illustrious dead. For, from the earliest age the corpse was an object of solicitude; it was expected to have a revival of the vital spark. No sooner had the wail of anguish passed the lips of those that loved it, than the grim ministers of embalmment took it into their keeping. The paraschistes or dissector opened the side with an Ethiopian stone, the viscera and softer parts were removed; the body was soaked in various salts steeped in liquid resins, and even boiled in wax or bitumen. No pains were spared to make it retain the outward appearance of its living form. Bandages of linen were then carefully wound around it, and hundreds of yards packed it with pledgets into a symmetrical shape. It was then consigned to its coffin or sarcophagus, gaily painted or elaborated, sculptured with appropriate mortuary scenes and funeral prayers, accompanied with the paraphernalia of the tomb, the boxes, jars, and other objects deposited for its use.

The service of the dead was then performed. Hired mourners chanted dirges, or simulated the tears, the groans, and cries of grief, tore their hair or beat their breasts, in pantomimic woe. Transported to the barge, the Egyptian hearse, it floated down the Nile to the site of some favorite cemetery—to the Pyramid fields of Memphis—the sepulchre of Osiris at Abydos—or the rocks of Gournah in the Theban quarter. Even the litanies or masses continued to be said at intervals as long as families could pay, or the local priesthood pray; and the tombstone invited the passer-by to recite a brief formula for the dead that he might enjoy all the good things of this life in the future state, pass in and out of Hades, and the soul transmigrate as it wished.

The political constitution of Egypt appears to have consisted in a territorial aristocracy of nobles, at the head of which was the monarch, and a powerful priesthood, with richly endowed temples, in possession of the literature and learning of the race. The king was considered a kind of Sun on earth, and was supposed to be descended from the gods themselves. At his coronation he was anointed; and his birth, purification, or baptism, and death, were thought to be presided over by the gods. His power was absolute or nearly so, but in the civil administration he was assisted by princes, royal scribes or secretaries of state, intimates or counsellors, and privy counsellors, who had right of access to the royal presence. One of the highest officers of state, was the bearer of the flabellum at the right hand, who possessed a judicial authority. For the administration of criminal law in cases of high treason and other crimes, commissions were appointed comprising the high officers of state, and there appears to have been a kind of council or ministry of thirty, who accompanied the monarch in his military expeditions. The monarch was head of the army, and the princes held high commands; besides them were generals called *haut*, colonels or *mer*, lieutenants *ten*, captains *ment*, and other officers. The drill of the forces was very regular, and the service severe. The army was divided into corps or brigades, which bore the names of different deities. It had standards, music, cars or chariots for transport, and all the necessary appliances for provisions, as well as catapults, battering rams, and scaling ladders for sieges, but all these were not in use at first; encampments were also constructed. At all times auxiliaries or mercenaries were in the service; Negroes, at first, and even later, Libyans, Sardinians, and Greeks, composed a considerable portion of the forces. The Egyptian fleet consisted of transports for the conveyance of troops, and when at a later period it came in conflict with the Phœnician and Greek it showed no great capacity for maritime war. It consisted of galleys with a single bank of oars: each had at least two officers, and during war military officers embarked on them and took the command. Besides war, the military acted as police, and special divisions for the purpose were attached to the palaces and the temples. The civil government was confided to special officers, who were sometimes hereditary. There was a duke or lord *ha*, of each nome or district, and under him a prefect *mer*, of each principal city, besides a magistrate *ga*, who heard civil plaints. "Auditors of pleas in the Tribunal of Truth," or judges, are also mentioned, as also the scribes or clerks, and the superintendents of servants of the same tribunal. In the time of the Ptolemies, and perhaps earlier, these judges made the circuit. Attached to the administration were scribes or clerks, who kept registers of the public property and drew up official reports, and superintendents of the different subdivisions of the royal stores and other property, as the magazines of corn, arsenals, wardrobes, horses, cattle, treasury, palaces.

Egypt swarmed with a bureaucracy, the mark of a highly civilized community and centralized government. The taxes appear to have been paid in kind and had accordingly to be received by the scribes and other officers of the Pharaoh. The palace had several officers attached to it, and one of the chief functionaries was the superintendent of the inner portion, perhaps the harem. The butler and baker of the palace are found on the monuments.

The priesthood was all powerful, and divided into several grades. At Thebes the high priest of Amen was second only to the king, and, as mentioned, ultimately ascended the throne. He was called the chief prophet, and four at least of the order were attached to the worship of Amen. Other deities and deceased monarchs appear to have had prophets only. Besides the prophets, was a lower order called divine fathers, and priests, *ab*. Inferior officers, such as servants and slaves, were assigned to the temples, while sacred scribes kept the accounts and performed the necessary duties of clerks. Although the Egyptians had not, strictly speaking, castes, yet the son often succeeded to the office of the father, while he could also become a scribe or military officer. All three titles are often found attached to the same person, showing that there was no strict limitation of hereditary succession. The offices held by women were necessarily few and chiefly in connection with the priesthood. Queens were honorifically styled wives or handmaids of the god Amen, and some females of high rank were prophetesses, singing women, and sistrum players of the god.

As festivals occupied a great portion of the second calendar, they had some occupation in the performance of the rites. The year consisted of twelve months of thirty days, making 360, to which were added five additional to raise it to 365 days; but it was then one quarter of a day too short, and lost one day every four years, returning to its normal condition after 1460 years had passed. All attempts to rectify it were either forbidden or else failed, although the change of the seasons, which were three—Spring, Summer, and Winter, showed the error of the vague or wandering year. Each day in this year was deemed lucky or unfortunate, and consecrated or devoted to some particular god. Attempts to substitute a fixed year, although often made, quite failed till the time of the Romans, when the Alexandrian year, beginning on the 20th of August, was substituted for the vague year. At the expiration of the Sothic cycle, the first of the month Thoth or New Year's Day, began on the 28th of July, coinciding with the first appearance of the rising of the Dog-star in the morning before the sun, and the commencement of the Inundation. In the festivals, the arks of the gods were carried in procession, sacrificial offerings were placed on the altars, and songs and prayers were sung or recited in honor of the gods. All religious rites were celebrated with great pomp, and supplies of food were consumed or given away on the occasions. The priests and their families drew rations from the temples, and the priests of the monarchs were supported at the charge of all the temples. The prophets were divided into four orders, and were promoted from one to the other, according to their ability or influence, and in the highest posts were elected by the chapters or synods. They were shaved, wore linen dresses, and papyrus sandals. Besides them there were many inferior servants and others attached to the service of the temples, and a kind of monks, who lived in the precincts. On matters relating to the temples, the contributions to the king and other affairs, occasional synods were held at different places. All things connected with the temples and worship were in the hands of the priests. The embalmers appear also to have belonged to the order of priests, although of inferior rank: they attended to the preparation of the mummies, sepulture of the dead, and recital of litanies. The bodies were not prepared in the houses of the deceased, but removed to public establishments of *choachytai*, as the embalmers were called. A certain custom prevailed of chasing the embalmer who cut the side of the corpse for the removal of the internal parts of the body. Hired female mourners assisted also at the last rites, when the mummy was deposited in the sepulchre, and mutes or priests with standards swelled the funereal cortege.

The Egyptian was in mind, acute, subtle, dogmatic, and egotistic. Fond of literature, the arts and sciences, he was obstinate to excess for gain, and prone to luxury. Neither devoid of courage, nor incapable of heroic effort, he was not equal in these qualities to his northern neighbors. His loyalty was slavish, his submission to his superiors servile, his piety tinctured with base superstition. His perception of moral truths and social duties was high; his inventive powers considerable; his conceptions of art stupendous. He influenced the thought of the neighboring nations. Moses was learned in his wisdom; the Hebrew dwelt with him; the infant Christ was carried to him; and the great doctrines of Christian faith were established by him when he had assumed the garb of Christianity, and thrown off the slough of Paganism.

HISTORY OF EGYPT.

CHAPTER I.

OLD EMPIRE.

FROM THE FIRST TO THE CLOSE OF THE SIXTH DYNASTY.

From about 3000 B.C. to 2000 B.C.

The first monarch of the country was Mena, or as he is called in Greek, Menes, and his name, the same as that of the bull Mnevis, of Heliopolis, appears to mean the firm or stable. He is supposed to have attributed his laws to Thoth. Later writers ascribed to him the introduction of luxury, and the corruption of manners if not morals; for Mena was supposed to have introduced a more refined civilization than the austere and simple mode of life which had preceded his reign. One of his successors, probably the most parsimonious of the royal line, ordered a malediction of Menes to be engraved on a tablet and placed in the temple of Amon-Ra at Thebes. The first laws of the country and the earliest rites of public worship were attributed to

Menes, but above all he founded Men-nefer or Memphis, the oldest, if not the most celebrated city of the empire. The dyke of Cocheiche, his great work, which still exists in the neighborhood of Cairo, rising to more than three feet above the level of the stream, was constructed by him to turn aside the current to the East, and protect from inundation the capital of the old monarchy. On the land thus obtained from the ancient bed of the river, Menes built the town, the fortifications, and the temple of Ptah, the eponymous deity of Memphis, which was called the Men-nefer or "Good Port," softened by Greek euphony into Memphis, and by the Copts to Memfi, a name still retained by the ruins of Tel-Monf. Two Arab villages, Mitrahenny and Bedrestein, are all that now attest the site of this ancient and vast city, a considerable portion of which still remained in the Middle Ages, until its ruins were used as materials for the construction of the neighboring town of Cairo. All that remains of the temple of Ptah, and that chiefly of the period of the nineteenth dynasty, lies deep under the alluvial deposit of the Nile. But the time of Menes was also one of that eternal war which never ceases in the history of mankind. He undertook military expeditions against the Libyans, but perished, devoured by a crocodile; these great saurians at that time descending the river to the very shores of the sea. No contemporary monument is known of his age, or inscribed with his name. This indeed is found placed at the head of the royal lists of dynasties at Sakkarah, Thebes, and in the papyrus of Turin; but nothing known to have been made at the time of Menes remains, and he must be placed amongst those founders of monarchies whose personal existence a severe and enlightened criticism doubts or denies. Menes was supposed to have been succeeded by his son Atahuti or Athothis, of whom nothing is known beyond the recorded fact that he built the royal palace at Memphis, and had written works on anatomy. Some of the oldest works on the healing art which have come down to the present day inscribed in the hieratic character on papyri, are attributed to the kings of the Old Empire. To that period must be referred the commencement of the art of embalming the dead, which required an empirical knowledge at least of the different parts of the human frame. The king Athothis was succeeded by another of the same name, and that monarch in his turn by a king named Ouenephes, in the Greek lists. During his reign Egypt was said to have been afflicted with a famine, and he built the pyramids at Kochome, or the town of the "Black Bull." This pyramid exists at Sakkarah, and is the oldest Egyptian monument hitherto found. It appears to have had a base of nearly 394 feet square, and rose to the height of 196 feet, with a slope or angle of 73° 30′. It was constructed of calcareous stone and granite, and had seven steps like the Babylonian towers, but had not the minute care and finish of the pyramids of the later dynasties. The pyramid was a royal sepulchre, a geometric mound erected to preserve the royal mummy, and a sarcophagus and some other remains were discovered in it when opened. Ouenephes reigned according to the canon only twenty-three years, and was succeeded by Hesep or Ousaphais, of whom little is known except that some religious and medical works are referred to the period of his reign, which lasted only twenty years. Probably one of the pyramids of Lower Egypt was his sepulchre, but modern researches have not discovered which of these numerous constructions were dedicated to the sepulchre of the royal mummy. After the death of Ousaphais, Miebies, called by the Egyptians Merba, mounted the throne. He reigned twenty years, and nothing of importance has been recorded of the events of his reign, nor any other monument than his name remains. Semempses, his successor, whose name is found both in the Egyptian and Greek lists, reigned for eighteen years, but the only recorded fact of his rule is the prevalence of a great plague. Bieneches succeeded him with a reign of twenty-six years, and with him closes the first dynasty of the eight Thinite monarchs who succeeded one another in the direct line, each the son of his father, for the space of 253 years, according to the summation, or 263 years according to the total of the years of their reign.

The second dynasty was also of Thinite monarchs, but as little is known of the events of their reigns as that of their predecessors. They appear, however, both in Egyptian and Greek lists, but with some difference of transcriptions, showing that some uncertainty about their appellations prevailed even amongst the Egyptians themselves. The first king Butau, or the Greek *Boethos*, is stated to have reigned thirty-eight years, the most remarkable event of the period being a fissure of the earth, probably the result of an earthquake, which carried off many people at the town of Bubastus. His successor Kakau, or *Khaiechos*, instituted the worship of animals, which prevailed so extensively at a later period. To him is referred the introduction of the Apis bull worshipped at Memphis, and the bull Mnevis at Heliopolis, as also of the goat *Baentattu* at Mendes. These animals were supposed to be gods, or rather a second emanation or terrestrial manifestation of the deities—Ptah Socharis, Osiris, a cosmic demiurgos, Tum or Tomos, the setting sun, and Chnoumis, the spirit of waters. Kakau reigned thirty-eight years, and was succeeded by Baienneter or *Binothris*. Another political change marked his rule; the law that females might succeed to the crown, which was clearly not the case in the hereditary male succession of the first dynasty, and his predecessors of the second. Binothris probably had no male heir, and thus endeavored to secure the crown to his daughter, who in all probability, if she did not die before him, succeeded to his power. He reigned forty-seven years. His successor, Utnas or *Tlas*, reigned seventeen years, and was followed by the King Sent or *Sethenes*, who is said to have reigned forty-one years. A monument, part of the architrave of the door of the tomb of a prophet attached to the worship of this monarch, exists in the Ashmolean Library at Oxford. In style, character, and treatment, it closely resembles similar sculptures of the period of the fourth dynasty, from which it does not differ in any essential particular; but it is remarkable as exhibiting at so early a date the introduction of the personal adoration of the monarch, supposed, according to Egyptian notions, to be the direct and lineal descendant of the gods, and of the same substance or flesh with them. This worship of mortals was extensively introduced into the religious system; and its priest or *flamen*, as the Romans called such officers, continued till the subjection of Egypt to the arms of Rome, and probably even later. Utnas was succeeded by a monarch named in the Greek lists *Chaires*, whose reign did not extend beyond seventeen years, and the Greek glosses mention the rule

Pyramid of Meydoum.

of these three monarchs as quite inglorious. Their successor was Neferka-ra or *Nephercheres*, who reigned forty-eight years, and in whose time the Nile is said to have flowed with milk and honey. His name occurs in the lists and on some scarabæi and other objects; but as there were several kings who bore the same appellation, it is difficult to tell to which they ought to be assigned. The monuments of this period are excessively rare, and almost limited to the tombs in the cemeteries of Gizeh and Sakkarah, and the pyramid of Meydoum. The first appearance of the word Ra or the Sun, occurs in these last two names, all the previous kings having been called by a simple or significant name. After this period the word Ra constantly appears in the royal titles or appellatives. Neferka-Sekar or *Sesochris*, was his successor, and reigned forty-eight years, or eight and a quarter only according to the papyrus of Turin. The Greek glosses state that he was five cubits or about ten feet high, and three palms or twenty-eight inches broad. Two or three different Egyptian names are recorded as those of his successors, but Manetho gives only Cheneres, an inglorious monarch with a reign of thirty years. About 300 years are assigned as the duration of the entire dynasty.

The two Thinite were succeeded by a Memphite dynasty of nine kings, the first of whom, Neb-ka, was the *Necherophes* of the Greek lists. He is said to have reigned twenty-eight years, but the statement that the Libyans revolted in his reign, shows that at a prior period they had been subjected to the arms of Egypt. A sudden increase of the moon's size, apparently a lunar eclipse which occurred at moonrise, so terrified the Libyans that they submitted again to the rule of Egypt. Neb-ka was succeeded by Ser or Serbes, the Greek *Tosorthros*, called by the Egyptians Aesculapius, who appears at a later period to be the god Aiemapt or *Imouthos*, the son of Ptah. He obtained this appellation on account of his knowledge or patronage of the medical art, and is stated to have invented the art of building with polished stones, and also to have given attention to the making of inscriptions or writings. Probably his age marked a higher development of these arts; but all these arts had been exercised under his predecessors. A long succession of inglorious monarchs, Tota or *Tureis*, with a reign of seven years, *Mesochris* with one of seventeen, *Souphis* with that of sixteen, *Tosertosis* of nineteen, *Aches* of forty-two, *Sephouris* of thirty years, and *Kerpheres* of twenty-six years, close the dynasty. Some of the kings had the Egyptian names of Neb-ka-ra and Huni, but with the exception of the last, who was apparently the *Kerpheres* of the Greeks, the names cannot be satisfactorily identified. The duration of the dynasty is given as 214 years. Besides the step-shaped pyramid of Sakkarah some other monuments are known of these dynasties. The tomb of Tothept in the cemetery of Sakkarah, three statues of the family of a person named Sepa discovered near the pyramids, two others with an European cast of features and attributed to the second dynasty, found at Meydoum, and at present in the Louvre at Paris, and the tomb and statue of Amten, an officer of the reign of Sephouris, are the principal monuments of the period. As the civilization of Egypt did not differ except in a slight degree from that which prevailed under the subsequent dynasties, the state of literature and the arts will be considered at the end of the chapter.

It is with the fourth Memphite dynasty that the history of Egypt begins to assume greater importance, the events recorded are no longer dependent for their remembrances on the glosses or curt notices of Greek epitomists, but the monuments of the country contain exact and contemporary accounts of the events which took place. The first monarch of the line was Senefru or the Greek Soris, if indeed that name does not represent another monarch. The most remarkable event of his reign was the discovery of the mine of *mafka*, supposed to be the turquoise at Wady Magarah, in the Peninsula of Sinai in Arabia, not far from the spot of the wanderings of the Israelites in that locality.

Pyramids of Gizeh. From the Nile.

A tablet at the mouth of the cave or ancient mine represents Senefru conquering one of the people named *Mena nu sat* or "Shepherds of the East," probably the nomadic tribes of the neighborhood, called at the period the Abt or Eastern land of Senefru. It is the first monumental record of Egyptian conquest. The names of different members of the family of Senefru are found in the sepulchres at Gizeh, and one of an officer named Amten, throws some light on the political state of the country. It records that some of his lands came to him by hereditary descent, while others were the gift of the monarch. Dates of reigns are rarely found on the monuments of the period, but Soris the first monarch of the dynasty is said to have reigned nineteen years. The successor of Senefru was Khufu or *Cheops*, probably the king best known in the annals of Egypt, on account of the great pyramid at Gizeh which was erected by him. This greatest of the world's sepulchres, on a base of 746 feet, rose to the height of 450 feet, more elevated than the Cathedral of St. Paul's, on an area, about that of Lincoln's Inn Fields; its former inclined height of the sides, which slope at an angle of about 51° 50′, was 611 feet, and it had two sepulchral chambers with suitable passages. The pyramids appear to have been called *mer*, or *abmer;* the origin of the word *pyramis* or "pyramid" being probably, like the other well-known word *obeliskos* or "obelisk," derived by the Greeks from words in their own language. The principle of their construction appears to have been the following:—Very early in the life of a king the surface of the limestone work was levelled for the base, a shaft more or less inclined was sunk leading to a rectangular sepulchral chamber in the rock itself. The distance from the entrance of the shaft or gallery to the chamber was calculated at the distance the square base of the pyramid would cover so as to exceed and not be overlapped by it. If the king died during the year the work was finished at once, but should he have lived another year a second layer of masonry was placed on the substructure of the same square shape as the base, but smaller, with the sides parallel to those of the base. The process went on year after year, each layer being smaller than the previous. When the king died the work was at once stopped, and the casing or outer surface of the pyramid finished. This was effected by filling up the masonry with smaller stones of rectangular shape, so that the pyramid still presented a step-shaped appearance. The casing of each triangular face was then smoothed from the top or apex, the masons standing on the steps and hewing away the edges of each row of stones as they descended to the base. When finished, the faces were perfectly smooth and the top inaccessible. Each of the casing stones capped the other so as to leave no vertical joint. The principle of the pyramid combined the power of increase in size without alteration in form, and its sloping side carried off the occasional rainfall without allowing the water to penetrate the building. Simple in shape it was eternal in duration, and exhibited a perfect mathematical knowledge of the square and the triangle. All pyramids were not constructed exactly alike; the older one of Meydoum, already mentioned, is constructed with rubble and slanting walls, but the idea of shape and the mode of finish are really the same. The size of the pyramid depended in a great degree on the length of the king's reign; but it is evident that those monarchs who desired to excel their predecessors in the magnificence of their sepultures could carry on the work on a large scale and more rapid manner, by the expenditure of greater riches or by the oppression of *corvées* or forced labor, which has prevailed at all times in Egypt. The material of which they were constructed varied; the nummulite limestone of the neighboring Arabian chain of hills was employed for the great mass of the work, but the granite of the distant quarry of Syene, principally the red, was used for casing the passages and some constructions of the great pyramid. It is by far the most remarkable of all the pyramids, for several changes appear to have taken place during its construction. The first or subterranean chamber appears to have been abandoned in consequence of the prolongation of the passage extending beyond the base, the pyramid having continued to be built for a longer time than originally contemplated; a second chamber, called the queen's, with a pointed roof was then made in the masonry of the pyramid sixty-seven feet above the level of the base, and had a horizontal passage for 110 feet in the masonry communicating with the original passage, by a passage sloping at an angle with it. Finally the king's chamber or main one, the last made, with flat roof and four chambers of construction placed above, the last, triangular to lighten the weight of the masonry, was approached by the same passage as the queen's chamber, much enlarged and cased with red Syenitic granite, terminating in a horizontal passage with granite portcullises which were also to defend the entrance. The chamber was ventilated by air-shafts, and had in the centre the plain but royal sarcophagus of the builder of the pyramid. The stones of the chambers of construction had still scrawled in red ochre upon the name of Khnum-Khufu or Cheops, accompanied by other marks which the masons had scrawled upon them in the quarries. The ostensible use of the pyramid was for the sepulchre of the monarch. The causeway for the stone was built by a corveé of 100,000 men, relieved every three months for ten years, or in all 4,000,000 of men, and twenty more years at the rate of 360,000, giving 7,000,000 more men, were employed in the pyramid itself. So much exhausted were the resources of the monarch that ridiculous stories were told about it, and the monarch on account of the hatred the work produced was obliged to be buried in a subterranean chamber encircled by the waters of the Nile.

But not only in ancient but modern times have the pyramids been an enigma. They are alluded to in the book of Job as the desolate places, *haraboth*, which kings and counsellors of the earth built for themselves—and occult reasons have been given for their construction. It has been supposed that they were built to record an arc of the meridian, the earth's diameter, the revealed unit of measure, the exact rise of the old polar star α Draconis, and other points of cosmic or mathematical knowledge. These ideas do not appear to have entered into the minds of the constructors of the pyramids, who employed measure for their symmetrical construction; while there is no reason to believe from the monuments that the Egyptians knew the figure of the earth or more than the simplest astronomical facts of observation, the points of the compass and other elementary points of terrestrial or sidereal knowledge. Even the heliacal risings of Sirius or the Dog-star are not found recorded at this early period. The actual rule of Khufu did not extend beyond the peninsula of Sinai in Arabia; and a tablet at the mouth of the mine of the Wady Magarah records that Cheops continued the search for mafka carried on in that locality. The titles only of Khufu are found on the tablet there erected; but Khnum-Khufu appears striking down one of the prostrate enemies of Egypt, the Pet or An foreigners, in the presence of the ibis-headed god Tahuti or Thoth, a sufficient refutation of the statements about the impiety of Cheops, and the assertion that he did not worship the polytheism of the country. The tombs around the great pyramid are those of the princes and other members of the family or time of Khufu. Amongst them are those of a prince named Khufu-Shaf, and in their inscriptions is mentioned the wife of Khufu, whose name unfortunately has not been found. The most remarkable notice of his reign is on a tablet coming from Gizeh and now in the Museum of Boulaq. It states that Khufu found the Temple of Isis, ruler of the pyramid near the Temple of the Sphinx, on the north-west of the Temple of Osiris, Lord of Rusta, and that his pyramid was either built near the Temple of Isis, by himself, or that his daughter, the Princess Hentsen, built the pyramid at that spot. Khufu, it states, dedicated it to Isis and Athor, placed the inscription on the tablet and provided it with sacred food, built the temple of stone and replaced in it the figures of the gods. The Temple of the Sphinx lay, it appears from other inscriptions, to the south of the Temple of Athor, and north of that of Osiris. This Temple of the Sphinx was subsequently found by Mariette, and had been partly touched by Caviglia. If this inscription was contemporaneous with Khufu it would prove that the Sphinx was anterior to the fourth dynasty, but it does not appear to be so, and it is consequently doubtful if this marvel of Egyptian monuments is not to be referred to a later age. Amongst the remarkable monuments of the age of Khufu are the granite sarcophagus of Khufuankh, a priest of Apis, of the white bull and a sacred heifer. These animals were probably the bull Mnevis at Heliopolis, and the cow of Athor at Athribis. Of the other works of Khufu little is known: the court was evidently at Memphis, and most of the works carried on there. It appears however from an inscription found at the temple of Denderah that the plan of the Temple of Athor or Venus on the site of the old Tentyris was due to this monarch. A hieroglyphic inscription states that the great foundation and restoration of the monuments was made according to the plan found on decayed writings of the king Khufu. Another account of the same plan places it in the mythical ages of the followers of the god Horus, a parchment or leather roll of that date having been found in a brick wall of the southern temple, built by the King Pepi or Phiops of the sixth dynasty.* A medical papyrus of the British Museum† also states that a recipe for the cure of wounds was found in the night, in the principal hall in the Temple of Tebmut, in the days of Khufu, in one of the secret or holy places of the goddess by a minister of the temple. It was discovered in the moonlight, and brought as a valuable discovery to the king. Khufu or *Cheops*, according to the Greek epitomists, wrote a work called "The Sacred Book," much esteemed by posterity, although *Cheops* himself was accused of impiety, and supposed to have endeavored to suppress the worship of the gods. Priests indeed were attached to his worship, but these *flamens* appear in the reigns of still earlier monarchs, and there is no reason to believe that *Cheops* substituted his own personal worship for that of the deities of Egypt. The most lasting monument of his fame is the great

---

* Duemichen, die Bauerkunde, Dendera, s. 15-19.
† Zeitschrift, fur ägyptische Sprache, 1871, p. 62.

pyramid. In the days of *Cheops*, sculpture had attained great excellence, and one inscription records the offerings of images of stone, gold, bronze, ivory, and ebony presented by Khufu to the gods. The pyramid of Khufu was called the "Splendor of Pyramids."

The successor of Khufu, according to the lists, was the monarch Ratatef or *Ratoises*, placed in Manetho after Mencheres, but monumental evidence gives Shafra or *Kephren*, the second Suphis or Chabryes. It was this monarch who built the small temple behind the great Sphinx. The temple itself was made of alabaster, or arragonite and syenite, or red granite. Shafra decorated the temple with statues of himself, in green basalt, remarkable for their admirable portraiture and execution. The second pyramid was the work of Shafra; it was not so large as the first, but of admirable execution, and revetted at the base with granite derived from the quarries of Syene. Shafra calls it the " Greatest of the Pyramids." It would appear that Shafra was married to a queen named Merisankh; their son, the prince Nebemakhut, was a *hierogrammateus* or sacred scribe, and secretary of state or privy counsellor of his father. Amongst other offices held by his mother was that of priestess or prophetess of the god Thoth, for at this time females were admitted to participate in the honors of the priesthood, which at a later period were denied to them. It seems possible that Merisankh was the daughter of Khufu, and that some other persons, whose tombs lie around the pyramid, were sons or relations of these Pharaohs; but it is difficult to assign their exact degree of consanguinity, and nothing is known of the events of the reign of Shafra, which was probably tranquil, and politically insignificant; the energies of Egypt being directed to the construction of one of these vast, but scarcely useful edifices, an immense sepulchre, by forced labor, and according to the legends, the closing of the temples of the gods. The successor of Shafra was Menkaura or Mencheres, the builder of the third largest pyramid at Gizeh, distinguished from the others by its granite base. Each side measures 384½ feet, and its perpendicular height is 218 feet; and like the preceding, Menkaura must have expended much time and labor in building it. Some account of the operations for doing so are found on a hieroglyphic inscription of an officer named Tebuhen, who lived in the reign of the monarch, but the text is unfortunately too mutilated to make out its contents. According to the legends, Menkaura was a pious monarch, who reopened the temples, and restored the worship of the gods, repealing the acts of his predecessors. Some color to this statement is given by the record of the inspection of the temples of the country made in his reign by the prince Hartataf, who found in the course of his tours, in one of the sacred edifices at Hermopolis, a brick on which was inscribed one of the chapters of the ritual written by the fingers of the god Thoth himself. During the reign of his predecessor Khufu, however, medical treatises had been found in the temples by the priests, as already previously mentioned, so that the services must have been continued by prior monarchs, and probably revived by Menkaura or Mencheres. The researches of modern times broke open the pyramid of this monarch, and discovered his coffin and remains. These had been already rifled in times long past, having been carried to the upper chamber of the pyramid, the body deprived of its bandages and ornaments, and its torn fragments scattered about the chamber. The outer sarcophagus or coffin of the king, was a plain one of whinstone, ornamented with the usual architectural devices of the period of the fourth dynasty. The inner coffin was of cedar wood, in form of a mummy standing on a pedestal. It had no paintings, but was of great simplicity, and had down it two lines of hieroglyphs, a prayer or address to Menkaura, taken out of a ritual or set formulary. It reads thus:—" Oh, Osiris, king of Upper and Lower Egypt, Menkaura, ever living, born of Nut (the goddess of the celestial waters), substance of Seb (the Chronos or Saturn of Egypt), thy mother Nut is spread over thee; she renders thee divine by annihilating thy enemies. Oh, king Menkaura, living for ever!" This inscription is remarkable, as showing that the worship of Osiris had assumed greater importance in the reign of Menkaura; for not only does the deceased king bear the name of that god, but the whole prayer refers to the myth of Osiris, his parents and his triumph over his enemies or accusers. Before the time of Menkaura, the god Anubis is mentioned in the tomb as the special deity of the dead, to the exclusion of the name of Osiris; but the coffin of Menkaura marks a new religious development in the annals of Egypt. The reign of Menkaura is given as sixty-three years, and he was succeeded by the king Shepeskaf or Aseskaf. A personage of the court buried at Sakkarah, in his sepulchre has recorded that he was brought up along with the royal infants, in the palace of Menkaura, and that the king Aseskaf continued to let him be educated in the palace amongst the princes. Subsequently Aseskaf gave his daughter, the princess Matsha, in marriage to Ptahases. The praises and honors rendered by the monarch to his son-in-law were considerable. He was invested with the post of secretary of the board of works, and the king allowed him to go into the royal palace without prostrating himself in the presence of the monarch. Besides which he had the privilege of entering the sacred barge of the gods, apparently a royal honor. The numerous offices that he held show that pluralities were of a very early date, unless it is to be conjectured that he held them in succession. But the kings of Egypt accumulated the different posts of the priesthood on the members of their family, or the personal adherents of their court. These posts entitled them to draw largely on the royal and sacerdotal revenues, while the great variety of functions exercised by the select few show a highly artificial state of society, already enslaved by an all pervading bureaucracy. The sense of public order appears highly refined at this early period, of public liberty there is no evidence. Civilization, in its sense of material prosperity, had no doubt attained, as will subsequently be detailed, to a considerable point. Under his reign the posthumous worship of his predecessor Khufu was continued, and a person named Shepeskaf, living at the period, was prophet or flamen of that monarch. The name of this monarch has been compared to that of *Asychis* of Herodotus, the successor of *Mencheres* or *Mykerinos*. There is some probability that this conjecture is correct. He reigned twenty-five years.

At the time of the fourth dynasty Egypt had attained a high degree of civilization; architecture as represented by the pyramids had become an advanced science, and reflected the geometric and theoretical knowledge of mathematics which their form and structure described for all future ages. The technical masonry was unrivalled, the finish admirable and unsurpassed by any later efforts of the Egyptian architect. The hardest materials, such as the granite of Syene, was hewn into the requisite form of the truest proportions, while the softer but more beautiful alabaster had been discovered and worked. In sculpture a canon of proportion had been discovered, and laid down for the human figure, and granite, durite and other hard stones conquered and moulded into shape by the efforts of the chisel. The statue of Kephren is equal, if not superior, to the subsequent efforts of Egyptian sculpture, while in the features is clearly to be recognized a portrait of the monarch, showing that the power of producing excellent representations of the living form in all its details existed. The other sculptures of the period exhibit even greater skill; the statues and busts in calcareous stone show a freedom of treatment and design which does not reappear in the more conventional forms of the later dynasties. The seated scribe in the Louvre, and the heads of some priests of the period are excellent examples, and rival in their portraiture the busts and statues of Rome itself. In wood even greater excellence was attained, for in that material the sculptor developed all his power. The wooden statue of the Museum of Boulaq is an unrivalled work of ancient art. It represents a person of high rank of an age after the meridian of life, with a truth, grace, and fidelity which shows the hand of a great master. The limbs are detached, the eyes inlaid, and in its lifelike treatment the experienced eye beholds the unchanging type of the inhabitant of the valley of the Nile. The bas-reliefs of the tombs are executed with a minute detail. The figures are severe and with great regularity of pose, without much action and always in profile; the eyes full, limbs, especially the hands and feet, large. Besides the ordinary flat bas-relief, the *cavo rilievo* or usual Egyptian bas-relief appears, the figures sunk in bas-relief below the surface which thus protected them from decay; a kind of union of the cameo and intaglio. The use of monochrome colors, principally red, black, blue and yellow, prevails, and is the only painting known of the period. The graphic system of writing was complete; the language perfectly represented by the hieroglyphs, which presented to the eye a lively picture on the painted wall of tomb or sepulchre; while the inscriptions show that the religion of the country was already reduced to a system, and the seasons marked by a regular calendar of festivals. The political organization had also attained a considerable degree of refinement. The Court of Memphis swarmed with sacerdotal personages, prophets and prophetesses of the gods, and priests attached to the personal worship of the monarch. Scribes and secretaries were attached to the Pharaoh, superintendents were set over every branch of the public service. In private life the Egyptian lord led a charmed life—his estate was cultivated by slaves, his household full of domestics; the barber, the waiting-maid, the nurse appear as necessary adjuncts to his household, as the steward who presided over the distribution and the clerk who checked the expenses of his daily life. Each priest or noble had in his establishment all the trades necessary for his ease and comfort; the glass-blower, the gold-worker, the potter, the tailor, and baker, and the butler. His leisure or *ennui* was charmed by the acrobat and the dancer, the harpist and the singer; games of chance and skill were played either by him or in his presence. The chief occupation of the period, or at all events that most often represented in the tombs, was the inspection of the farm. The noble of the fourth dynasty was a great hereditary landed proprietor. He had the pride of a patriarch in his flocks and herds, his numerous slaves or servants, his household of artizans and his boats on the great river Nile. His domesticated animals were not so numerous as at a subsequent period. He had dogs, cats and apes, for his companions. For riding he had only the ass, with the horse he was unacquainted, nor had the wheeled carriage as yet been invented. The gazelle, the antelope, the ibex, the leucoryx, varieties of the gazelle family of ruminants were known to him, as also was the ox, the short, long-horned, and hornless varieties. An Egyptian lord no more disdained the hyæna for food than a modern epicure the semi-carnivorous bear, but he abhorred that universal animal the pig, and neglected the sheep; veal and beef, not pork and mutton, were the principal meats that appeared at his table. The different kinds of venison already mentioned were much prized, and the chase of these animals one of his most loved occupations; of the birds of the air and water fowls he had a choice about as numerous; cranes and herons he sometimes ate, but his principal poultry consisted of different kinds of ducks and geese, the chenalopex or vulpanser amongst them. The domestic fowl was unknown to him, it had not been brought by the hands of tributaries to the valley of the Nile, where it never appears in Pharaonic times. The dove and the pigeon, however, passed into the fleshpots of Egypt. The insipid fish of the Nile were not unknown to him. His bread was made of barley, but conserves of dates and various kinds of biscuits or pastry diversified his diet; and of fruits he had grapes, figs, dates; of vegetables the papyrus and onion and other greens. Wine and beer were both drunk at the period in addition to milk and water. His dress was simple, consisting of pure white linen, but gold collars, bracelets and anklets were in use. As yet he wore no sandals, but he carried a wand or walking-stick as a sign of dignity or authority. Simple but elegant furniture ministered to his requirements. Stools, chairs, footstools, couches and head-rests or wooden pillows—the use of these rests is still retained in Africa—appear in the furniture of his elegantly-built house. The principal flower was the lotus nymphæa, for there were no roses in those days in Egypt. The lotus was held as a nosegay in the hand, and twined as a garland round the head, or wreathed the wine and the water vase. He enjoyed all the pleasures of existence, and delighted more in the arts of peace than war. In his religious belief the idea of a future state, and probably of the transmigration of souls, was ever present to his mind, while —and his long life was one preparation for death— to be devoted or pious to the gods, obedient to the wishes of his sovereign, affectionate towards his wife and children were the maxims inculcated for his domestic or inner life. Beyond that circle his duties to mankind were comprised in giving bread to the hungry, drink to the thirsty, clothes to the naked, oil to the wounded and burial to the old. On the exercise of good works he rested his hopes of passing the ordeal of the future and great judgment, and reaching the Aahlu or Elysian fields and Pools of Peace of the Egyptian paradise. Such was the ideal of a good Egyptian, and the favorable side of the picture; the other is not detailed, but may be imagined. To what it led will appear in describing the later dynasties. It is sufficient to show here, from the positive information the monuments afford, the point to which at this remote period the intellectual and material civilization of Egypt had advanced.

The transition from the fourth to the fifth dynasty took place from causes which have not been detailed. The dynasty was called Elephantine, probably from its founder having been a chief of the modern site of Geziret-Assouan. He was named Userkaf or *Ousercheres.* Little is known of his reign, and the most important personage of it, was Khnumhotep, who was priest of the goddess Athor, and of the pyramid of the king; but it is not known in which of these edifices he was buried, after an inglorious reign of twenty-eight years. He was succeeded by Sahura, or *Sephres* of the lists, who renewed the conquest of the Wady Magarah, and is there represented on a rock tablet striking down the Mentu foreigners, perhaps some of the tribes of the neighborhood of the great mine. Some of the tombs of Sakkarah record persons who existed under his reign, and his name, traced in red on one of the blocks of the pyramid to the north of Abusir, shows that he was interred in that monument called the *Sha ba* or "Rising Soul" pyramid. Priests attached to his personal worship are found as late as the Ptolemies, and his reign of thirteen years was more distinguished than that of his predecessor. Placing aside the monarch *Kaka*, who is only known from some lists, the successor of Sahura was Neferarkara, the Nephercheres of Manetho. Little is known of the events of his reign, except that several functionaries of his reign were buried in the cemetery of Gizeh; they were principally scribes and other functionaries attached to the finances and public works. Like his predecessors, he was interred in another pyramid after a reign of twenty years. The successor of this monarch was Ra-en-user, surnamed An, the Rathoures of the Greek lists. Under this monarch the mining operations at the Wady Magarah were continued, and a rock tablet on the spot records his name and titles. From the inscriptions in red ochre on the blocks of the middle pyramid at Abusir, that monument it appears was the sepulchre of his royal mummy. The tombs of this period in the cemeteries of Memphis are remarkably fine and numerous, and indicate a long reign. The lists give forty-four years as its duration. After the king *An* came Menkauhor or Mencheres II. Like his predecessors he continued the explorations at the Wady Magarah, and, as appears from the inscription, made an expedition in that region. In excavating the Serapeum at Memphis a slab was found with a representation of this monarch. He appears to have been youthful, with a good profile and rather a full face. The hieratic papyrus of Turin containing a list of all the kings before the twentieth dynasty, gives him a reign of eight years, and his legends show that he was another of the pyramid builders, although that in which he was buried is not known. His successor Tatkara or Tancheres also continued the mines at Wady Magarah. His surname was Assa. He sent commissions to examine the state of the locality and excavations in his fourth year. It appears that a god, apparently Thoth, had caused the precious *mafka*, the supposed name of the turquoise, which ran in their strata, through the serpentine rocks of that spot, to be discovered by a tablet which the god himself had written. The mine, however, it has been previously shown, had been found in the days of Senefru, and is always described in the inscriptions on the spot as belonging to that monarch, so that this account must refer either to the original discovery or another special indication of the lost vein, recovered in the days of Assa. Many and magnificent tombs of the period are found in the vicinity of Memphis, but the important monument of his reign is the papyrus called the Prisse, after its possessor. It is written in the hieratic characters, and the oldest extant document in this frail material. The author of the composition, Ptahhetp or *Phthaophis*, was the son of a king; but was already overcome by old age at the moment when he reduced to writing his moral precepts or book of Egyptian wisdom. It was written, according to the author, "to teach the ignorant the principle of good words, for the good of those who listen, to shake the confidence of those who wish to infringe." It is supposed to be addressed to his son, and in language which calls to mind the wisdom of Solomon, Ptahhetp says, " With the courage that knowledge gives, discuss with the ignorant as with the learned; if the barriers of art are not carried, no artist is yet endowed of all his perfections. Good words shine more than the emerald which the hand of the slave finds on the pebbles." The duty of filial piety is strictly inculcated. "The obedience of a docile son is a blessing; the obedient walks in his obedience. He is ready to listen to all which can produce affection; it is the greatest of benefits. The son who accepts the words of his father will grow old on account of it. So obedience is of God, disobedience is hateful to God. The heart is the master of man in obedience and disobedience, but man gives life to his heart by obedience." The idea of filial obedience is repeated in many forms. "The rebel who obeys not," it says, "does really nothing; he sees knowledge in ignorance virtue in vices; he commits daily and boldly all sorts of crimes, and lives as if he were dead. What sages know to be death is his daily life; he goes his way loaded with a heap of curses. Let thy heart," it adds, "wash away the impurity of thy mouth. Fulfil the word of thy master; good for a man is the discipline of his father, of him from whom he has sprung. It is a great satisfaction to conform to his words, for a good son is the gift of God." The dissertation ends: "It is thus I obtain for thee health of body and the favor of the king, and that you pass through your years of life without falsehood. I am become one of the ancients of the earth. I have passed 110 years of life by the gift of the king, and the approbation of my seniors, fulfilling my duty to the king in the place of his favor." These extracts show the wisdom of the Egyptians in which Moses was said to be versed, and which were an ancient code of morals in his time. They recall to mind ideas found in the sacred writings, as the age of the writer does that attained by Joseph in the land of bondage, who lived 110 years, a period often alluded to in Egyptian inscriptions of a later time, as the extreme limit of human life; long life being esteemed one of the blessings vouchsafed to obedience and those favored of the gods. Unas or *Onnos* closes the list of the monarchs of the fifth dynasty, and little is known of the events of his reign. It has been supposed that he gave his name to the city of Unas in Middle Egypt, and his son-in-law, Snatemhat, has left behind him a magnificent tomb at Gizeh. The name of Unas is not found at the Wady Magarah; but several small objects inscribed with it, probably derived from the tombs at Gizeh, are in the different museums of Europe. He reigned thirty-three years, and was buried in the long building constructed of enormous blocks of limestone, anciently inlaid with hard stones at Sakkarah, and known at the present day by the name of the *Mastabat-el-Faraoun* or "Pharaoh's board." His name has been found upon a stone near the entrance. With Unas the fifth dynasty closes; and it appears from the papyrus at Turin, which marks a total in the rubric before his name, that his reign was one of those fixed points from which the ancient Egyptians computed the chronology of the old monarchy.

The sixth dynasty which succeeded has been termed Memphite, but some have considered that it was probably Elephantine. There was some connection with the local worship of that site in the time of the fourth, as the name of Khnum, the local god of Elephantine, appears attached to that of Cheops. The monuments of the sixth dynasty are found extending farther south into Middle Egypt than those of its predecessors. Its first monarch, Teta or *Othoes*, was said to have been killed by his guards, although the reason is unknown. He is said to have reigned thirty years. Abeba, an officer of his reign, whose tomb has been found at Sakkarah, mentions that he accompanied the king in his voyages to the edifice of the South, and had access to the inner palace or person of the monarch, and that the king, who esteemed Abeba more than any of his other courtiers, supplied him with food on his journeys. The monuments of the dynasty now begin to appear at El Kab or Eileithyias, Hammamat, and Abydos, which last became one of the burial places of the contemporaries of these monarchs. The successor of Teta was Pepi or *Phiops*, also called *Mira* or *Merira*, whose reign the epitomists have placed at 100 years, but this is proved by the monuments to be too long and inexact. A tablet at the Wady Magarah, dated the fourth of the Egyptian month Mesori, the last of the year, and the eighteenth year of his reign, records the examination of the mines by a commission. Pepi had to reconquer the Mentu, who inhabited the peninsula, in his second year. Considerable light is thrown upon the events of his reign by the inscription of a priest and officer of the court named Una, found at San or Tanis. This officer was crown bearer, while a youth, to the king Teta, who had made him superintendent of the storehouses, while under Merira or Pepa he became chief of the coffer, and the prophet or priest attached to the pyramid or sepulchre of the monarch. His first mission was to the land of Ruau, in the South, whither he was accompanied by an officer and company of soldiers to transport thence the royal sarcophagus, and the jambs and lintels of the door of the royal pyramid. Companion of the king, privy counsellor, secretary of state, he subsequently rose to be a general, and carried on a campaign against the Aa or Aamu, some of the Asiatic neighbors of Egypt and the Herusha "those in the sands" or desert, supposed by some to be the Arabs. For that purpose he levied an army of *Nahsi* or negroes, from the Ethiopian lands of Aruret, Aman Uauat, Kaau and Tatam. These negroes, then first mentioned in history, were officered by Egyptians, some of whom were priests. Una prepared the commissariat and the sandals, and made several incursions on the Herusha. He burnt the strong places, cut down the vines and fig trees, slaughtered many of the enemy, and led back several prisoners as the result of his victories. The subjection of the foe was evidently incomplete; the enemy concentrated again at the land of Takheba, and Una, re-embarking his forces, again marched against the Herusha, giving them a signal defeat in the north of their territory. This has been supposed to be some part of Eastern Egypt or Arabia, for the exact country of Herusha has not been determined. It is possible that Una sailed to it by sea, although that term is not mentioned, and Una may have only embarked on the waters of the Nile. In reward for his distinguished services Una had the privilege of wearing his sandals when he entered in the palace, the rewards and decorations of a later age not having at this time been adopted. The pyramid of Pepi was called Mennefer, the name of Memphis; probably it was one of the group at Gizeh. He was married to a queen named Rameri Ankhnas, and succeeded by their son Merienra. The reign of Merienra, successor of Pepa, appears not to have been very long, but not the less distinguished. The king had ascended the Nile, as far as the cataracts, and an inscription on the roads of Assouan records his safe passage and return.

The officer Una, whose inscription has been already mentioned, lived in this reign. He was appointed chief and governor of the South from Elephantine to the second nome, and sent by the king to get the sarcophagus and part of the original sepulchre or pyramid from the land of Abeha, and the granite door from Elephantine. He went for the purpose with six transports, six other boats and a vessel of war, and reached a point where no Egyptian had arrived before. He also removed from the quarries of Hatnub or Ombos a large sepulchral altar of alabaster, in the short space of seventeen days, and excavated four basins or ports in the land of Uaua to hold his transports. The negro chiefs of the lands of Arurat, the Uaua, the Am, as tributaries of Egypt, supplied the wood necessary for this work, which occupied the space of one year. At the time of the inundation he loaded his vessels with granite for the royal pyramid, and he built chapels in honor of the spirits or protecting genii of the king, in each of the four ports. It is clear that there was some difference in the state of the Nile at that period. Neferkara, or Nephercheres I. successor of Merienra and his brother, continued the works at the Wady Magarah. A commission in the second year of his reign has recorded its arrival on the spot. They consisted of twelve persons, at the head of which was the chancellor Hapi. The captain of the boat who appears in the former commissions, is not mentioned, and the party may have come by land instead of crossing the Red Sea. He is the last king recorded on the spot. The papyrus of Turin places Nitakar or Nitocris, the celebrated queen with "rosy cheeks," before Neferkara. According to the Greek legends, to revenge the assassination of her brother, she invited the conspirators against his life to a feast in a chamber lower than the level of the Nile, and then turned the water of the river upon them. After her death she was said to be buried in the third pyramid. Some insignificant names follow Nitocris, whose absence from the monuments proves that her reign was not of length or importance. The difficulty of reconciling the monumental and traditional information and dates has given rise to several chronological schemes. It is sufficient to state that the dynasty flourished about 200 years.

With the sixth dynasty closes the period of the grandeur of the old monarchy, and the mode of life and civilization described at the close of the fourth apply equally to the sixth dynasty. No temples of the period remain. The monuments are all sepulchral, and the tombs are all constructed on the same plan; they consist of massive and square chapels, where the relations of the dead and priests assembled and performed the liturgies on the appointed festivals. From the chapel a well descended vertically into the soil, and at the bottom of the well was the vault or tomb, in which the mummy lay deposited in a granite sarcophagus or wooden coffin. The process of embalming was a mere pickling or salting, and the body but slightly bandaged. The adornment of these chapels was also uniform; there were more figures than inscriptions, and the subjects were derived from private life. No gods are seen on the walls, although their names were known and their forms sculptured on the historical or political tablets. The name of Osiris begins to appear. Sculpture is admirably shown in the statues of the period, the arts and sciences had visibly advanced since the fourth dynasty. At this time the neighboring countries were plunged in a comparative state of barbarism, and held by wandering tribes, not more relatively, advanced in arts and sciences than the Bedouin of to-day. There may have been the commencement of a parallel civilization in the valleys of the Tigris and

Euphrates, and the germs of a more spiritual religion in the wandering families who drove their flocks and herds on the skirts of these regions. But as yet the patriarch Abraham, the believer in the One and true God, had not appeared on the scene, and there was no link which connected the Egyptian with the Hebrew. After the sixth dynasty a monumental gap, which as yet can neither be filled up nor bridged over, occurs till the eleventh dynasty.

CHAPTER II.

MIDDLE EMPIRE.

FROM THE SEVENTH TO THE EIGHTEENTH DYNASTY.

From about 2000 B. C. to 1600 B. C.

THE official lists of the kings inscribed on the walls of the temple of Osiris at Abydos and at Karnak, in the tombs of Gournah and Sakkara, and the papyrus of Turin record many monarchs that belong to this obscure period. A few amulets and other objects offer also isolated names, but no monument of importance attests their sway. It has been supposed that such may hereafter be found at Meydoum, Lisht, Ahmes-el-Medineh, or the zone of land which bars the entrance of the Fayoum. It is difficult to believe that for a period of 436 years, given by the epitomists as the interval of time that separates the sixth from the eleventh dynasty, Egypt should have been ruled by a foreign race, invaded by an unknown people, or offer no proof of national existence. The seventh or eighth Memphite dynasty are supposed indeed to have been contemporary with the ninth and tenth Heracleopolite. This reduces the period to 285 years, but does not solve the difficulty. The eleventh dynasty comprised eight kings, who bore the names of Antef or Enantef, and Mentuhetp or Mandouophis, and appear to have been established only in the Thebaid. No monuments of importance dated in their reigns are known, and the sepulchres of the family are in the valley of Assasif or the western valley at Thebes, built of unburnt brick, and ornamented with their tablets and inscriptions. From their names being alternately Antef and Mentuhetp, it is probable that they continued in a direct unbroken succession. The coffins of two of the Antefs, made of single trees, and their mummies, enveloped in the pasteboard envelopes called cartonages have been found. Antef I., the first of the family, was embalmed by his brother Antefaa—or the "Greater Antef" as he is called. The tomb and tablet of Antefaa have been discovered in the valley of El-Assasif at Thebes. On it he is represented standing amidst four dogs, each of a different kind, and wearing a collar, and accompanied by its name. The king is followed by the master of his hounds. The tablet is stated in the inscription to have been set up at this pyramid or tomb in the fiftieth year of the reign of Antefaa, and when at the time of the twentieth dynasty the sepulchre had been attempted by plunderers and violators of tombs, it was discovered and recognized by this tablet. Antefaa was no doubt a mighty hunter, as the dogs are hounds and used in the chase of the gazelle and other animals. Mentuhetp II., the fourth king of this Theban line, appears on the sculptures of the rocks of the island of Konosso near Philæ as the conqueror of thirteen nations, probably of the South. He adores the god Ammon Horus, who, under the name of Khem, was supposed to be at the same time Ammon the chief of the Theban gods, and Horus the son of Osiris, one of the inferior deities of Abydos, the ancient Madfouneh-el-Arabat; for the Egyptians in their polytheism often united together two different deities or invested them with each other's attributes. This type of Ammon and Horus was the protector and chief god Coptos. This town, named Kebta, and from which the Coptic language derives its name, and even, according to some writers, the name of Egypt itself was formed or invented, was under the eleventh dynasty an important fortress commanding the entrance of the valley of Hammamat; and amongst the numerous inscriptions which cover the face of the rocks of that spot, it is recorded that Coptos was the residence of Mentuhetp, and that the votive inscriptions were in honor of the god Khem who dwelt in "the beautiful valley" of Hammamat. One of the most remarkable is dated in the second year of the reign of Mentuhetp III., the sixth king of the eleventh dynasty. In it he states, "My master the king, Mentuhetp III., the ever-living, sent me as a commissioner, for I am of his sacred family, to set up the monuments of this country. He selected me from his capital city, and chose me out of the number of his counsellors. His Holiness ordered me to go to this beautiful mountain, with the soldiers and principal persons of the whole country." Here it will be observed that the monarch is spoken of in terms more applicable to a god than a mortal, and is invested with an official title of sanctity such as the predecessors had affected, who had even priests attached to their personal worship. It is such pompous and vain epithets that hardened Pharaoh's heart and made him consider himself a god, or at least equal to one. The commissioner was not only accompanied by troops, but also by masons, sculptors, and others employed in making monuments to Khem the lord of the quarries in the mountain. In the same year another inscription of the same purport, announcing that the king, Mentuhetp III., had ordered the same to be engraved on the rock in honor of his father, the god Khem, lord of the mountain districts of the valley. The architect employed was also accompanied by troops to protect or watch the masons and laborers employed in the quarries. They continued to work at the quarries of green breccia and dark granite, which supplied the materials for the temples and other Egyptian edifices of the period. A person who lived in the reign of one of the Antefs was buried in the reign of Usertesen I. of the twelfth or succeeding dynasty at Abydos, thus connecting the two families and proving the succession of the twelfth dynasty; and at a later period the tombs of the Antefs are recorded in Egyptian monuments, especially one at which was the sepulchral stelé or tombstone of the king standing amidst his dogs, who had their names inscribed above them. The civilization and the arts of this period so closely resemble those of the subsequent dynasty that they will be considered with them. The first monarch of that line was Amenemha I., who seems to have risen after some political disturbance to the throne. He reigned nine years alone and seven associated in the government with his successor Usertesen I. A few monuments of his reign are in the temple of Karnak, which he appears to have commenced, and in the quarries of Mokattam, near the modern village of Toura, in the neighborhood of the ancient Memphis, and those of Hammamat, which were still worked. A papyrus in the British Museum records the instructions given in a dream by Amenemha I. to his son; as far as it can be made out the life of the monarch was attacked possibly by his son Usertesen I. Amenemha describes it in his good deeds, how he had sent his commissioners and couriers to Abu or Elephantine and Athu or Natho, hunted the lion and crocodile, fought against the Uauat or negroes, led captive the Magau, and built himself a magnificent palace, probably at Heliopolis.

His successor, Usertesen I., appears to have been principally occupied with the conquest of Kush or Ethiopia, of which he has left a record on a tablet inscribed with the account of his victories at the Wady Halfa in Nubia. He conquered eight of the principal tribes of the neighborhood and his conquests assured to Egypt a long rule over Ethiopia, which remained for many years a dependency of Egypt. In a tomb at Benihassan a person named Ameni, who died in the forty-third year of the reign of Usertesen I., has left an account of the exploits he performed and the service in which he was engaged. Ameni it appears was an Egyptian general and governor of Sah, as the sixth canton or nome of Upper Egypt was named. At the head of a picked body of troops, 400 in number, he had marched to the gold mines of the South and accompanied the king in a campaign against the Ethiopians, the limits, as he calls them in the inscription, of the world itself. The division of the army to which he was attached was under the command of the prince and heir apparent Ameni. He had escorted from the gold mines the booty or produce to the fortress of Coptos, and with such skill and success that he had not lost a single man in the operation. On another occasion he had marched at the head of 600 troops, the élite of the district, for the same purpose. In addition to the spoil or produce of precious metal which Ameni had obtained from the South, he had also acquired 3000 head of cattle, probably from Kush or Ethiopia, which abounded in herds, especially in those of the zebu or humped kind; and according to his epitaph, he had acted both as agent, steward, and administrator of the district. From the royal workshops he had never, it states, abstracted anything. He worked diligently, and the district was full of life and activity. "Never," it says, "was any little child ill-treated by me, never was any widow afflicted by me. I never troubled a fisherman, or hindered any shepherd. I never took away the men belonging to a person who superintended a gang for my works.

There was not any famine in my days, and no hunger under my government. For I worked all the fields of the district of Sah to its frontiers on the South and North; I kept the inhabitants alive by offering its products, so that there was none starved in it. I gave equally to the widow and the married woman, and did not show preference to the great and not to the little ones in what I gave. When the Nile made a great inundation I did not cut the branches from the channel." This remarkable inscription recalls to mind the famines to which Egypt was occasionally subject owing to a deficient Nile. Such a famine happened in the days of Abraham amidst the neighboring nations, and he then went to Egypt, which then, as at a later period, was the granary of the adjacent countries.* It also shows that there had been about the period years of famine like the seven years of which Pharaoh had dreamed† in the vision of the seven lean kine, supposed by some to be the same as the seven mystical cows of Athor, the goddess of beauty; which, according to the interpretation given by Joseph to the Egyptian monarch, meant seven deficient years. It is also remarkable that in the tombs of Abydos at this period were buried several overseers of the account of the corn placed in the royal granaries; the mention in the hieroglyphic inscriptions of these officers, suggests that years of famine had caused them to be appointed for the purpose of providing against a future calamity. In the advice given to Pharaoh, he was told to "appoint officers

* Gen. xii. 1-10. † Gen. xli. 54.

F.

over the land, and take up the fifth part of the land in the seven plenteous years, and to let them gather all the food of those good years that come, and lay up corn under the hand of Pharaoh, and let them keep food in the cities."* Besides the superintendents of the royal granaries, scribes or clerks were also appointed, who took charge of the accounts of the corn. Some of these accounts of a later period have been handed down, and from them it appears that the corn was threshed about a month after it had been gathered into the garner. It was piled up in heaps there, and must have been often turned, but when transported was carried either in sacks or baskets. From the cakes which have come down, the Egyptians appear to have principally eaten barley bread. Another kind of barley, or "red corn," as it was called, was employed for beer, which is made in Egypt till the present day.

In the thirty-eighth year of his reign Usertesen I. associated his successor, Amenemha II. in the government, and reigned four years longer. Very little else is known of his reign except the wars in the South against the negroes, the extraction of gold from Nubia, and the fortification of the fortress of Samneh, to curb the incursions of the black races. An officer of the two kings during their joint reign attended to the station of the land of Uaua, one of the tribes on the Nile, close to the Egyptian frontiers. On the North the king had not advanced farther than the peninsula of Sinai, where the mines

* Gen. xli. 34, 35.

still continued to be worked. At this time Egypt was under a territorial aristocracy, which received its titles and investiture from the Egyptian king. In the tombs of Benihassan one of these great lords or princes records the history of his family, and his investiture with the government of Menat-Khufu or Minieh. His name was Khnumhetp, the son of Nehara and a lady named Bakat. The family of Khnumhetp claimed to be descended from the gods of Memphis, and Amenemha II. had appointed him governor of the Eastern districts. His mother had been created a princess by her marriage with Nehara, who held that rank and was a governor of the country. In consequence of his station, Amenemha II. had raised the son Khnumhetp to the rank of chief of the district of Menat-Khufu or the modern Minieh, in the nineteenth year of his reign. He had continued the dignity to the family; and from other sources it appears that Khnumhetp had been employed in the mining operations at the Sarabit-el-Khadim in the peninsula of Sinai and Magarah. Although works were carried on at the Wady Magarah till the forty-fourth year of the reign of Amenemha II., the veins of turquoise and copper having become exhausted at that spot, the explorations of the Sarabit-el-Khadim were commenced in the twenty-fourth year of the reign of Amenemha.

The most remarkable representation sculptured on the walls of the tomb of Khnumhetp is one in which certain Amu or Semitic foreigners are depicted arriving at his court and ushered into his presence. So striking a resemblance does this scene bear to the arrival of Jacob in Egypt that some have seen in it a picture of that event. As the number of persons mentioned is not the same as accompanied the patriarch, and the names and conditions differ, it can only be considered to represent a similar scene. The men are represented draped in long garments of various colors, and wearing sandals unlike the Egyptian, more resembling open shoes with many straps. Their arms are bows, arrows, spears, and clubs. One plays on a seven-stringed lyre by means of a plectrum. Four women, wearing fillets round their hair, garments reaching below the knee, and anklets, but without sandals, accompany them. A boy armed with a spear walks at the side of the women, and two children seated in a kind of pannier placed on the back of an ass, precede the women. Another ass, carrying spear, shield, and pannier, precedes the man playing on the lyre. The number of the foreigners is of course different from the sixty-six of the family of Jacob which came down to Egypt; and other tribes and nations, as the Midianite merchants to whom Joseph was sold, and carried him to Egypt as a slave, came to that country. But the scene so strongly recalls the arrival of the family of Jacob in Egypt, with a scene such as the entrance of the Hebrews into Egypt probably presented at the time. Khnumhetp receives the foreigners accompanied by one of his followers, who carries his sandals and a staff, and is attended by three dogs. A scribe, named Neferhetp, unrolls a letter or papyrus, in which it is stated that thirty-seven Amu have come to Khnumhetp. An inscription over their heads records that the picture represents the bringing of the mestmut, or kind of stibium by thirty-seven Amu to the Egyptian governor. The features of these strangers are like that of the Jews, and their dress differs from the Egyptian. The men wear each a single garment of divers colors such as Joseph is said to have had; and the chief named Abusha, has one richer than that of his companions, ornamented with a fringe and a meander border round the neck. In his left hand he holds a short stick or crook, and with his right he offers a he-goat, seven others follow with their asses and their children. The Amu, is however, the general appellation of the Semitic races, and there is no indication of the particular tribe of that great family.

Usertesen III. constructed the fortress of Samneh on the south of the Wady Halfa, close to the second cataract, to curb the incursion of the negroes of Kush. This town formed at the time the limit of Egypt on the South, and a tablet of the eighth year of his reign forbade any negro to pass it, except in the boats conveying cattle, oxen, goats and asses, and things belonging to them. These were either required for the support of Egypt or permitted to return to the frontier; but all other boats were forbidden to enter the port on the Nile called Heh. The king also set up his statue at the same spot. The pressing affairs of his reign seem to have been the necessity to hold Ethiopia under his sway. Like his predecessors,

Usertesen still continued to work the quarries of basalt at Ruhannu or Hammamat, to which an architect had been dispatched in his fourteenth year, while no notice occurs of those of the Sarabit-el-Khadim. He reigned thirty-eight years, and was subsequently deified by Thothmes III. in the temple at Samneh, and festivals appointed to be held in his honor. His successor, Amenemha III., was not distinguished by any foreign conquests, but seems to have undertaken the great construction of the Lake Mœris, one of the most stupendous works of the Old Empire. It would appear that in his reign some disturbance had taken place in the annual inundation of the Nile. It has been already shown from the monuments of his predecessors, that Egypt had suffered from the effects of famine, probably from the inundation not having reached the height of the number of cubits requisite to fertilize enough of the soil for the support of its inhabitants. The prosperity, almost the life of the country, depended on the regularity of the inundation. Should the water of this greatest and most mysterious of the rivers of the ancient world attain too great an outpour, instead of fertilizing with their unctuous deposit the desert which girdled them, they destroyed the labors of the husbandman and the hopes of the harvest. On the other hand, if they became like the lean kine of Pharaoh's dream, too little to form a broader strip of land than the river's bank, a barren year of famine was the necessary consequence to the teeming population clustered on the banks of the father of the gods and the hidden or mysterious water of Egypt. Impelled by these considerations, Amenemha III. began the construction of a gigantic lake on the West of Egypt; it was fed by a canal from the Nile, diverted the superfluous water of an excessive Nile, so as to regulate its overflow, and hoarded those of a deficient Nile to spend them as required on the neighboring land. Besides its use for irrigation it also contained an immense quantity of fish, from which the Egyptian government derived a large annual revenue.

In the second year of his reign the mines of the Wady Magarah were still worked under the command of an officer who occupied the spot with a garrison of 734 men. The place was occupied by troops and miners till the forty-fourth year, or the close of the rule of this monarch. But the operations at the Sarabit-el-Khadim went on at the same time, where there was erected a temple of the goddess Athor, who presided equally over the copper and turquoise veins of the neighborhood. The commissioners and officials sent to the district, recorded on the rocks their valuable services; that they had pierced the hill and thrown light on its hidden treasures. One states that he went on foot through the secret valleys of the place, records the arrival and submission of the foreigners of the district, and the quantity of material he extracted from the mines. More important than the mines of Mount Sinai were the engineering operations connected with the course of the Nile, which it had become necessary to regulate by sluices and reservoirs. Anciently the inundation of that great river, the father of waters, had irrigated and enriched the soil of Ethiopia or the modern Nubia, and indications of its old bed still remain in the alluvial plains of that country, but in the days of Amenemha III., some great displacement or change had occurred. The years of famine mentioned in the previous reign had probably their origin in deficient Niles or inundations. In the fourteenth year of the reign of Amenemha, the condition of the Nile attracted unusual attention on the part of the government of the Pharaohs. Commissioners and other officers were sent down to Samneh to examine, report, and mark the height attained by the river. It was nearly twenty-four feet higher than it reaches at the present day. Some have indeed supposed that the Nile broke a passage through at Silsilis at a subsequent period, and that the bed was consequently lowered. At all events the king found it necessary to go on with the constructions of the celebrated lake known to the ancients as the Lake Mœris, the modern Birket-el-Faraoun, lying on the South-east of the Fayoum. Availing themselves of a natural depression of the land, and by damming up the gorges by dams, the Egyptians formed an artificial reservoir of water, which communicated with the Nile by a canal called the Bahr-el-Jusef, open when the Nile was at its height, and subsequently closed as the river retired to its bed. The water thus obtained was secured in the reservoir by sluices, and retained during the dry season when it was let out to irrigate the lowlands of the neighboring districts.

Besides finishing the Lake Mœris, the same monarch also constructed a pyramid at the corner of the lake for his sepulchre, continuing the mode of burial used by the monarchs of the fourth dynasty. The base of that pyramid has been discovered in recent times, and blocks of stone inscribed with his name and that of a queen his successor. But the greatest edifice which he built was the Labyrinth, consisting of a number of small chambers communicating with one another. According to Herodotus it contained 600 chambers, or rather passages, 300 of which were above the level of the ground and as many below. The object of this singular edifice was stated to be for the reception of the princes and other dignitaries of the country. It preceded by centuries the celebrated one of Gnossus in Crete, in which king Minos kept the monster called the Minotaur, half man, half bull. This Cretan work consisted of a series of meandering passages, in which the intruder, who had not the requisite clue, lost himself and fell a victim to the monster who dwelt within. Probably some reason of suspicion and security caused the construction of this singular building, which, with the pyramids and obelisks, was another marvel of Old Egypt. In Egyptian, the Labyrinth was called Mera, and had the same name as the lake. The same word was also applied to streets, which probably in Egypt originally did not run in straight lines as at present, but followed a tortuous or meandering course. The pyramids, for there were two on the borders of the lake, are supposed to have had colossal statues of the kings at their summits; and the king for this purpose as early as the ninth year of his reign, had begun to draw materials for their construction from the quarries of El Hammamat. He also despatched thither architects, to obtain from the quarries the stones of requisite size. In the time of Herodotus, who visited Egypt in the reign of Darius, or about B. C. 445, the Lake Mœris, its pyramids, and its Labyrinth, were still existing, although they are now an almost indistinguishable mass of ruins. The Labyrinth greatly astonished this ancient Greek traveller. It had, according to his description, twelve courts, all roofed with stone, which was unusual in Egyptian buildings, most of which had no ceilings, and were open to the sky or *hypoethral*, as the Greeks called them. It had twelve courts, with gates exactly opposite one another, six facing the north, and the same number the south, and a great number of chambers, according to the account of Herodotus, 4500, above and below. The subterraneous chambers or crypts Herodotus did not see, but he heard that they comprised the tombs of the kings who built the Labyrinth, and those of the sacred crocodiles which were attached to the temple of Sebak the crocodile god, of Crocodilopolis or Crocodile Town. These great reptiles were exceedingly tame, and wore ear-rings, and the Labyrinth seems to have been their sepulchre, although the principal pits in which the mummies of the crocodile are found are at Manfalut. The courts of the Labyrinth had colonnades and entrances into the various chambers. The whole was surrounded by an outer wall, and the walls covered with hieroglyphs; but little is known of the purport of the inscriptions, and the mere fragments which have been found contain the titles only of two kings. At one of the corners of the Labyrinth stood a pyramid, forty-one fathoms, or 246 feet high, which was entered by a subterraneous passage. Two other pyramids stood in the centre of the lake, 300 feet high above the surface of the water, which was of the same depth at this spot. On the apex of each of these pyramids was a seated colossal figure. These three pyramids were the sepulchres of the kings. The Greek account gives different names to the king of the Labyrinth; but the fragments of it which have been found near the walls of the crypts or subterraneous chambers, show that it was Amenemha IV. and his sister, whose mummies were perhaps buried in the pyramids placed in the middle of the lake, which, according to some, was so called from the name of the king who made it; and as his prenomen or divine name was Mænra or Mara, it is of course just possible, although the explanation given before is considered better than that the lake derived its name from the monarch. Nor is it impossible that the lake itself was made to protect the pyramids, for Cheops was said to be buried in a chamber surrounded by the water of the Nile, and the whole mind of the kings was directed to construct these gigantic monuments of human vanity, more than to the improvement of their people and public works of a greater utility.

In the reign of Amenhetp IV. the mines at the

Wady Magarah continued to be worked and new ones opened. One of the king's officers states that he arrived there with fifteen men and worked diligently, and that the produce of his labor exceeded that obtained in the days of king Senefru, while other tablets set up on the spot record the quantity of cattle and fowl, and the journeying of the troops there, for the Peninsula was unsafe without military escort. On another tablet, apparently about the same period, an officer states "to the miners that if you fail, Athor," that is the goddess who presided over the district and the mines, "will hold out her hands to help your workmen in the work: look at me, how I waited there after I left Egypt, my face sweated, my blood was heated." The vein did not appear to yield at first, but after a time a good quantity was extracted from it. All this took place at the Wady Magarah and Sarabit-el-Khadim, close to Mount Sinai, many centuries before the Israelites crossed the desert and came to the adjacent spot.

From some unknown reason after the twelfth dynasty, Egypt had again declined, and another monumental gap marks the interval between the twelfth and eighteenth dynasties. The thirteenth is said to have been Theban or Diospolitan, but the fourteenth was from Xois or Sakha. It has been conjectured that nearly a thousand years intervened between the close of the twelfth dynasty and the expulsion of the Shepherds; but there is no temple or monument of importance to mark the interval. The extraordinary number of sixty kings attributed to the thirteenth dynasty, and of seventy-six to the fourteenth, is unparalleled in the annals of any country. The monarchs that are known are called Sebekhetp and Mentuhetp, and the repetition of names resembles the system of the previous dynasties. Statues and tablets of some of these monarchs have been found at San or Tanis, Harabat-el-Madfouneh or Abydos. These monarchs of the thirteenth dynasty held Egypt from Nubia to the Mediterranean as sole monarchs. Sebakhetp IV. like the kings of the eleventh, recorded the height of the Nile at Samneh, from the first to the fourth year of his reign at the fort Khemu of Usertesen III. Another king, Neferhetp, and his family are registered on the rocks of the island of Shel at Assouan and Konosso. A statue of Sebakhetp lies in the island of Argo, and at Thebes and Hammamat other memorials of the dynasty appear. Nothing certain is known of the fourteenth dynasty, and it is probable that at the commencement of its sway Egypt was invaded by the Hyk-shos or Shepherds, and the native monarchs driven to the South. The Shepherd kings are said to have easily subjected the country, burnt the towns, devastated the temples, ill-treated the Egyptians, and reduced their wives and children to slavery. The name of Hyk-shos appears to mean "ruler," *hyk* of "Shepherds," or "Nomads," *Shasu;* and the invaders to have been some of the Arab or Semitic tribes, thrown by movements in Central Asia on the borders of Egypt. The first prince of the line, named Saites, is said to have built the city called Avaris, on the East of the Bubastite branch of the Nile. Some of the names of the monarchs have been found in the lists and on the monuments, that of Saites or Set on a tablet at San, and several monuments of Apepi or Apappos on the same spot: at Tel-el-Yahoudeh, and Mit-Fares in the Fayoum. The Shepherds, it is stated, established their court at Memphis, garrisoned and rendered tributary the entire country. The course of time, however, weakened their power, and the native princes who had withdrawn were enabled to resume the offensive against the foreigners and finally expel them from the country. It is indeed apparent that the rule of the Hyk-shos did not extend much beyond Memphis, and that the Egyptian monarchs held Thebes, the nascent capital of the country. The papyrus of the British Museum, so often cited, details the circumstances of the quarrel. "The country of Egypt," it states, "fell into the hands of the lepers, and no one was king of the whole country. For the king Rasekenen was only king of Upper Egypt. The lepers were in Heliopolis, and their ruler Raapepi at Haouar or Avaris. The whole country was tributary to him, making complete service to him, for it brought him all the good productions of Lower Egypt. The king Raapepi chose the god Sutech as his lord, and was not the follower of any other god in the whole country. He built him a temple existing forever." Subsequently it is stated the Shepherd king sent a herald or an ambassador to demand workmen and materials of the Egyptian prince, to build the temple of Sutech or Set. The king assembled his council and refused. Here the document prematurely ends. It does not appear that Ra-sekenen was strong enough to expel the Shepherds, for a naval captain named Aahmes states that in his youth he dwelt in the fortress of Eileithya, and that his father at the time was lieutenant of the king Ra-sekenen. As he was afterwards in a subsequent reign present at the siege of Avaris, it is evident operations had not commenced.

The arrival of Joseph in Egypt has been placed by some in the reign of Apepi II., and some considerations are very favorable to that conjecture. The name Potiphar, from its composition, is evidently Heliopolitan rather than Theban. Joseph married the daughter of the high-priest of Heliopolis, occupied by the Shepherds during their occupation of the country. No mention is made in the narrative of Memphis or Thebes. The 430 years of the bondage of Israel in Egypt correspond with the monumental date of 400 years from the Shepherd rulers Set or Saites to Rameses II., and the opinion generally entertained by Egyptologists, that the Exodus took place in the reign of Meneptah, son and successor of Rameses II. The elevation of a foreigner to the high office held by Joseph, is also more consonant with Egypt being at the time in the hands of the Hyk-shos, while the Pharaohs of Heliopolis must have known the patriarch, whose eventful story would have been unknown to the native dynasty, which expelled from the soil of Egypt the hated Hyk-shos, their traditions and antecedents. This will be reconsidered when the period of the Exodus comes under consideration. The tomb of the Ra-sekenen or Sekenenra, whose name was Taakan, as it appears, was at the Drah Abu-el-Neggah, in the Assasif or western valley at Thebes, where, however, it has not yet been discovered amongst those of the kings of the eleventh dynasty. The names of individuals who lived at the period just before and at the commencement of the eighteenth dynasty, are repetitions of those which appear in the eleventh and twelfth, proving that they belonged to the same families, and were probably not separated by any great interval of time.

CHAPTER III.

NEW EMPIRE.

FROM THE EIGHTEENTH TO THE TWENTIETH DYNASTY.

From about 1100 B.C. to 1600 B.C.

THE fall of the Shepherds gave rise to the eighteenth dynasty, and the war begun by Taakan ended by the final expulsion of the foreigners, and the extension of the Egyptian frontiers to the banks of the Euphrates and the Tigris. Discarding the different lists mutilated or disguised by Greek transcription, the first monarch of the dynasty was Aahmes or *Amosis*, who was raised to the throne of Upper Egypt, and who appears to have wrested ultimately Northern Egypt from the hands of the invaders. The king Taakan held his Court at Eileithya, but Aahmes evidently possessed Thebes at the commencement of his reign. The naval officer Aahmes, already mentioned, states that in the reign of Aahmes he was lieutenant on board the vessel called "The Calf," and that he served in the Northern fleet, which was evidently engaged in transporting the Egyptian troops to the seat of war. He marched on foot at the side of the war-chariot of the king, and was present at the siege of Ha-uar or Avaris. He then embarked on another ship called Shæmmannefer, and was present in some naval actions on the waters of Ha-uar or Avaris, by which must be understood the Tanitic branch of the Nile. Aahmes brought thence the hand of a dead enemy, which, in accordance with the usages of the period, he had cut off, as a proof of his prowess, and the king presented him with the decoration of a collar of gold. In a second action he exhibited the same valor, and obtained the same reward. In a third engagement, which took place at the south of Avaris, he took one of the enemy prisoner, dragging him through the water in the direction of the fortress, and, embarking him on his vessel, carried him off. For this deed of valor he received the special recognition and thanks of his sovereign. At the capture of Avaris he took prisoner a man and two women, whom the king gave him for slaves. From this it is clear that Aahmes completed the recovery of Egypt Proper, and succeeded in restoring the national dynasty to its old superiority.

After the capture of Avaris, the king besieged the town of Sharuhana or the later Sharuhen of the tribe of Simeon * for six years, and took it. At this siege Aahmes again distinguished himself, and took two women as prisoners, and one hand which he had cut off an enemy whom he had killed. The king gave him the customary reward of a gold collar, and the captives for slaves.

Subsequent to the defeat of the Shepherds, the monarch turned his attention to Ethiopia, probably on account of some revolt or incursion which the

---

* Joshua xix. 6.

negroes from time to time made on the Southern frontiers of Egypt. He prepared an expedition against *Khenthannefer* or "The Port of Good Return," already mentioned in the inscription of Una, and signally defeated the Nubians. Present at that engagement Aahmes took two prisoners, and cut three hands off enemies, whom he had killed in a personal encounter. He received the prisoners as slaves, and the collar of gold. Not only does this inscription throw light upon the external politics of Egypt, but also on the national character. The Egyptians were not deficient in courage, while the prisoners of the North and South, dragged into the households or workshops of their masters, must have given rise to a mixed race, that modified the national type and character. The negro, mentioned at the time of the sixth dynasty, does not appear in any of the sculptures of the tombs as actually employed in the service of the house or the labors of the field. At the eighteenth dynasty the negress mounts the throne of Egypt, and, as will be subsequently seen, intermarried with the sovereigns, whose features, as beheld in the sculptures, recall their mixed origin. After the expulsion of the Shepherds and defeat of the Nubians, Aahmes devoted his attention to the restoration of the temples, which had fallen into dilapidation, or been destroyed. The twelfth dynasty had founded several small temples at Thebes, the Wady Halfa, and elsewhere. Aahmes, in the twenty-second year of his reign, opened the limestone quarries at Mokattam, for the repairs of the "Temple of

Millions of Years," or the Palace of the Hephaisteum, dedicated to the god Ptah, at Memphis, that of Amon-Ra at Thebes, and other monuments which the king had dedicated to the gods. The blocks of stone were placed in sledges, and so transported part of the way. The monarch reigned twenty-five years. His wife, called Aahmes-Nefertari, was a negress, and apparently the daughter of an Ethiopian monarch. The circumstances of his alliance are unknown, but in this he probably had only followed the examples of his predecessors; who, forced by the Hyk-shos to the South, had contracted marriages with the families of Ethiopian rulers. Aahmes was buried in the western valley of the Drah Abu-el-Neggah, in a tomb amongst the monarchs of the twelfth dynasty. After his death his widow appears to have held the reins of sovereignty during the youth of his son Amenhetp I., who seems to have been quite a boy when he succeeded to the crown. The principal officer of his reign was probably Aahmes, already mentioned. He conducted the vessel of the monarch to Ethiopia, to "extend the frontiers of Egypt," showing that, secure on the Northern frontiers, Amenhetp meditated the conquest of the South. The king captured the chief of the hostile Nubians, and Aahmes killed two of the enemy in the action—their hands he presented to the monarch. In his pursuit of the cattle and men, the great attraction for these facile invasions of the South, he took a prisoner, but does not appear to have received him as a present from his master. He sailed back with the king to Egypt in two days, from a place he calls "The Upper Well." The monarch gave him another collar of gold. Aahmes also captured two female slaves, besides those he had already brought to the king, who, as a recompense for his services, created him warrior of the king. Besides these exploits in the South, Aahmes had fought in the North the Amou-Kahak, and brought thence three hands of slaughtered enemies. In this reign the horse is first represented on the monuments as forming part of the chariot of the king, and the wheeled car is first seen. At the time of the fourth and fifth dynasties, the ass only was employed for transport, and the carriage consisted of a kind of seat, on which the rider sat strapped between two asses. At the later period of the twelfth, children were carried in a kind of pannier on asses. The ass however was not ridden; but the horse, first mentioned in the reign of Aahmes, and seen in that of Amenophis I., continued to be used for chariots, riding and ploughing during this and the following dynasties. Amenhetp reigned thirteen years and was buried amongst the kings of the eleventh dynasty. He was succeeded by Thothmes I., who directed his arms towards Nubia, and advanced on the land of Khenthannefer. His conquests of the South are recorded on tablets, dated in his first year, on the rocks of Assouan or Syene, and another in the quarries of Kerman, opposite the isle of Tombos, in the 19° of North latitude. Ivory, gold, slaves and cattle, appear to have been the chief attractions which invited the Egyptian arms to the South. The officer Aahmes, whose exploits extended later than Thothmes I., narrates that Thothmes came back to Thebes after having attacked the Ruten or Syrians, who are mentioned for the first time in Egyptian history. Thothmes also approached Naharaina or Mesopotamia, slaughtered several of their troops in battle and brought back numerous prisoners. In this expedition Aahmes, at the head of the troops, manifested his usual valor, and captured a chariot and its pair of horses. He received for this exploit the recompense so often mentioned. Thothmes continued the building of the Temple of Karnak, repaired by Aahmes, and placed two obelisks of red granite before the temple of the god Amon at that site. Like Amenophis I., he was worshipped after his death, and priests were attached to his worship. He probably reigned a short time, although the lists of Manetho assign to him a duration of thirteen years. After his death Thothmes II. ascended the throne, and reigned conjointly with his sister Hasheps or Hatasu. The events of the period are involved in mystery. According to some, Thothmes was married to Hasheps, or at all events under her tutelage. Hasheps assumed male attire; and probably one of those revolting conspiracies and family quarrels of the palace is veiled behind the fact of the short and inglorious reign of Thothmes II. After the death of her brother she ruled alone, and the principal event of her reign was the sending of a fleet to Taneter "The Holy Land," or Arabia Felix, and Punt, either the Regio Barbarica or Arabia.

The expedition was of a peaceful nature, to collect the marvellous productions of the country; and the representation of it on the monuments recalls to mind the voyages of the fleets of Solomon at a later period. The galleys of thirty oars and sails traversed the *Uatur*, or Red Sea, and returned laden with gums, scents, incense trees, ebony, ivory, gold, emeralds, stibium, cynocephali and baboons, panther skins, horns, and work-people. An old and fat queen of the country is represented on foot, walking after her husband, who receives the Egyptian leader. At the return of the expedition the queen chose some of the best scents, and prepared a cosmetic which breathed a divine odor, and made the skin like gold and ivory, and bright as the stars. Punt was one of the countries supposed to be under the jurisdiction of Athor the goddess of beauty, and the appropriate land of the requisites of the female toilette. Its inhabitants were, however, despised by the Egyptians, and termed, "ignorant" or "no men," probably from their unwarlike nature.

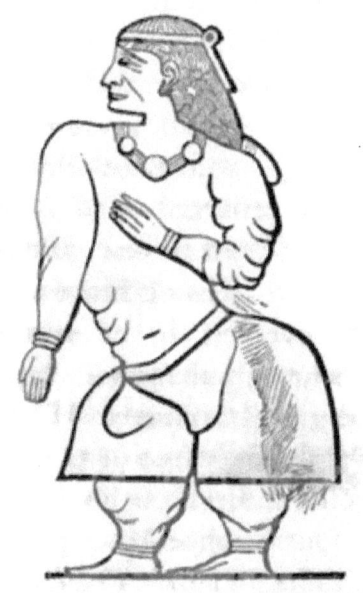

Arabian Queen in the Reign of Hasheps.

On the arrival of the convoy at Thebes the Arabians were received with honor, and the queen rejoiced at her successful enterprise and the acquisition of the precious gums and trees, which were planted in Egypt. It was the first time the land of Punt had been penetrated by the envoys of Egypt. In the Arabian queen may be seen one of the predecessors of the queen of Sheba, whose visit to Jerusalem plays so important a part in the history of the power and wealth of Solomon, when Sheba came with camels bearing spices, gold, and precious stones. At this period indeed the camel does not appear amongst the domesticated animals of Arabia, but only the ass, and although the Egyptians mention the natives of Punt in such depreciating terms, the handles and tools in use show that they had attained some degree of civilization. As will be seen, they continue to be mentioned amongst the tributaries to the Pharaohs. The name of Hasheps is often repeated on the monuments of Karnak, and she dedicated to the god Amon-Ra two great obelisks of Syenitic granite in honor of her father. They were placed at the doorway of the second court. These triumphal columns of Egypt were inscribed with hieroglyphical inscriptions, recording the praises, piety or exploits of the monarch by whom they were erected. Besides the inscriptions on the obelisks, the four sides of their pedestals also had records of the same queen. They state that the "queen, the pure gold of monarchs, had dedicated to her father, Amen of Thebes, two obelisks of *mahet* stone" or red granite, "taken from the quarries of the South;

their upper part," or "caps, were ornamented with pure gold taken from the chiefs of all nations." The inscriptions state that one day seated in her palace the idea had occurred to her of making two gilded obelisks, so high that the pyramidal cap of each should touch the heaven, and that she should place them before the pylon of Thothmes I. "Her Majesty," it states, "gave two gilded obelisks to her father Amen, that her name should remain permanent, always, and for ever in this temple. Each was made of a single stone of red granite, without joint or rivet. Her Majesty began the work in the fifteenth year of her reign, the 1st day of the month Mechir, of the sixteenth year, and finished it on the last day of the month Mesore, making seven months from its commencement in the quarry," or mountain. This proves that at this time the kings dated their regnal year from the day of their accession to the throne, and that the commencement of the queen's reign fell in the interval of the seven months mentioned in the inscription. Memorials of this queen exist at Medinat Habu, El Assasif, and elsewhere, allied with that of Thothmes II. At a later period she appears as co-regent with his successor Thothmes III., and takes precedence of him upon the monuments.

No document has preserved a record of the intrigues or discords of the palace which prevailed after the death of Thothmes II. ; but the disturbance in the public monuments which reflected the passions of the period, shows that some catastrophe like those which sullied the throne of the Ptolemies happened at this remote period. Hasheps at first, probably to conciliate public opinion, associated Thothmes III., then a youth, with herself upon the throne. The dedication of the statue of Anebni, a prince and military officer of the period, states that it was made by the orders of the queen Hasheps and her brother Thothmes III., for the deceased noble. The mines of the Wady Magarah, abandoned since the twelfth dynasty, were re-opened in the sixteenth year of the joint reign of Hasheps and Thothmes. A tablet in the Vatican, unfortunately not dated, shows the brother and sister invested with equal power. No later date is known of their joint sway, and the avenging chisel has obliterated her name out of every accessible monument of the country in which her title and authority were placed on a par with that of Thothmes. After the fall of his sister, Thothmes directed his attention to Asiatic campaigns; but how this bold ambitious woman fell does not appear, and the statues which remain of the queen offer none of those traits which announce great intellectual powers or exalted ambition.

The reign of Thothmes III. was the apogee of the greatness of Egypt. It is clear that he must have been a man of remarkable courage and capacity. Not only did he repulse the nations of the North and subject the tribes of the South, but he adorned Egypt and Nubia with magnificent temples and noble works of art. He appeared in person in the field of battle, and no consideration of personal safety or exalted grandeur retained him on the banks of the Nile while ambition and glory led his footsteps to the plains of Mesopotamia and the sources of the Tigris and Euphrates. The records of the reign of Thothmes are principally preserved at the sandstone wall which surrounds the granite sanctuary of Karnak, built by this monarch. It is there that he has recorded his expeditions or campaigns. The first of these he undertook in the twenty-second year of his reign, and in the month Pharmouthi he marched from Heroopolis, the Egyptian Garu or Taru, the frontier town of North-eastern Egypt with his army. On the month of Pashons of the next year of his reign he arrived at Gaha or Gaza; the date of the month is not mentioned, but it was the day of the anniversary of the festival of the coronation. On the 5th of the same month he marched from the town of Gaza to meet the enemy. On the 16th day of the same month he arrived at the town of Jaham, and marched thence towards Maketa or Mageddo, in the plains of which the enemy had concentrated his forces. Two roads were offered to his choice. The first and most direct passed by Aaluna, supposed to be Eglon, and Taunakas; the other passed by Tapheta or Gafta, and led to the north of Mageddo. The confederated kings in alliance against Egypt were the princes of Kharu or Syrians and the prince of Katesh or Kadytis; and on the 19th of the month Pashons of the twenty-third year the camp of the Egyptians was pitched at Aaluna. After a painful march Thothmes arrived at seven in the morning at the south of Mageddo, on the bank of the river or Lake Kaner. On the 22d of the month Pashons, three days after, the king engaged the enemy. "His majesty," says the text, "advanced in his gilded chariot, ornamented with wooden decorations, like the god Harmachis the entire lord, and Mentu of the Thebaid. His father Amen kept guard over the victorious exploits of his arms. The southern horn or wing of the army of his majesty was on the banks of the Kaina," the Lake Gennesareth, "and the north wing on the North-west of the town of Mageddo. His majesty was in the centre. Behold how his majesty attacked them. They fell," it continues to say, "prostrate in the neighborhood of Magarah through sheer terror; they quitted their chariots adorned with gold and silver, in which they were drawn, and fled in their clothes to the town of Maketa or Mageddo. When they reached that spot they were drawn up by their clothes into the fortress."

The Egyptian army it appears did not halt for the spoil, but continued to slaughter the enemy, who lay in ranks like fishes in a ditch. After the retreat of the confederated Syrian and Mesopotamian princes the troops returned to take the spoil, entered into the fortress of Mageddo, and appear to have either entrenched it with a palisade, or made another palisaded camp of wood in the neighborhood. The chiefs of the neighboring country tendered their submission to Thothmes; they came bearing gold and precious stones, and other valuables, and skins of wine, which the king ordered them to convey to the fleet. Amongst the captured spoil was the chariot of the king, and his brass armor, 340 captives, 2041 horses, 1920 oxen, 22,500 goats, and nearly 3,000,000 bushels of corn. Three fortresses were captured at the same time, named Inunamu, Anaugas, and Hurankal, which belonged to the Ruten or Syrians. The number of slaves, prisoners of war, and other persons captured, amounted to 2503, besides a considerable spoil of gold and silver vases, rings of gold and silver, chains, statues and other furniture, brazen vessels and garments. As far as Egypt was concerned, the victory at Mageddo opened to it the road to Central Asia. The annals of Thothmes are by no means complete, notwithstanding the accession to their details by inscriptions recently discovered. The subsequent years are however mentioned at Karnak. In the twenty-third and twenty-fourth year the Ruten or Syrians continued to bring their tribute, and Thothmes also received the same from Assur or Assyria. From this period there is a gap to the twenty-ninth year of his reign, which was the year of his fifth campaign. The king took some place, the name of which is too mutilated to make out, and the army congratulated the king upon it. From Tunep he took the prince or chief, 329 warriors, 100 *tens* or pounds of gold, besides vases of bronze and metal. The fleet of the king sailed to Egypt laden with the spoil. On his path he attacked the land of Areta, possibly Aradus, spoiled it of its grain, and cut down its trees. The land of Tahai, or Northern Phœnicia, also fell before his march. He "found the magazines full of corn, and the wine in their presses like waves." Their corn, it states, was in abundant heaps, and the army was satiated with the quantity of things it found there. The quantity of spoil in the expedition amounted to fifty-one slaves, thirty-two head of cattle, twelve silver cups, incense, balsam, honey, iron, lead, different kinds of precious stones, bread, barley, flour, and the soldiers had rations served out to them the same in quantity as during the festivals in Egypt. Although the inscription does not state it, the fact appears to be that Thothmes returned to Egypt. In his thirtieth year the king made a sixth expedition to the land of the Ruten or Northern Syria, one of the most civilized nations with whom the ancient Egyptians came in contact. The king approached the town of Kadesh, apparently the capital of the Ruten, and seated on the banks of the Arunata or Orontes. Kadesh was spoiled, the magazines were emptied of their grain to supply the Egyptian commissariat. From thence Thothmes marched to the towns Simyra and Arattu, and treated them in the same manner. The princes of the Rutennu or Syrians gave their sons and brethren to Egypt, and a particular number appears to have been kept up as a pledge of their submission, for the tablet states, if any of the chiefs died, his majesty made another come in his place. Their number is unfortunately wanting on the tablet; but 181 slaves, 188 horses, and forty chariots ornamented with gold and silver, were the spoil or tribute of that country. In the same year another place, named Hansatu, on the Lake Nesrana, was captured in an instant, and all the booty carried off. It amounted to 490 persons, twenty horses, and thirteen chariots with their harness. Hansatu must consequently have been an insignificant city or a small garrisoned fort. Indeed the inscriptions do not disclose in any instance places with a large population in this part of Asia. Besides the spoils obtained by military expeditions, the annual tribute still continued. The Rutennu or Syrian princes brought slaves, silver vases to the weight of 762 pounds, 19 chariots, 276 head of cattle, 4622 goats, which seem to have abounded in that region, hundredweights of iron, lead, armor, and rare plants, which were interesting to the Egyptian monarch or introduced into Egypt. The stations apparently of the route of the march of the Egyptian army were supplied with wine, honey, figs, bread, dates and other vegetable food. The quantity brought was inscribed on a roll in the palace, too numerous to detail on the inscription. On his return to Egypt the king was met by the Kanebti,* probably some of the neighboring tribes or colonists of Northern Egypt, for the tribute they brought was the gums and spices of Arabia. In that year also the tributes or embassies had been received from Kush or Ethiopia, especially the Uauat, who were nearest to the confines of Egypt; ten negroes for domestic servitude, 243 head of cattle, and boats

---

* Probably the "pillars" of the Egyytian state or principal officers. Compare Judges xx. 2; 1 Samuel xiv. 38; Isaiah xix. 13.

laden with tusks of ivory, logs of ebony, panther skins, and the other products of the country arrived. The Uauat amongst other things sent ninety-two head of cattle, and the herds of this part of the South, appear to have been offered as tribute to Egypt. They were the long-horned variety of domestic cattle, and the horns and tuft of hair on the head were, by artificial plaiting and carving, made to represent the fantastic device of the bust of a negro raising his arms as if in supplication; or bowls of water containing live fish were placed between their capacious horns. In his thirty-third year, the eighth campaign of this warrior king found him again in the land of Syria. His majesty approached a spot, either in Syria or the vicinity, where he placed one of those tablets which recorded the advance of the Egyptian army. Thothmes found already on the site a tablet of his father Thothmes I. Supposing that Syria is intended by the name of the Ruten, the place approached by Thothmes might be supposed to be the Nahr-el-Kelb or Lycus, in the neighborhood of Beyrout, and some of the tablets on the rock destroyed by the effect of time thought to be that sculptured by Thothmes I.; but as Thothmes soon afterwards passed into the land of Naharaina, or Mesopotamia, it is hardly possible that the Nahr-el-Kelb lay in the line of march. It is, however, the pass leading to Northern Syria, and the Egyptians, Assyrians, Persians, and Romans, traversed it on their passage between Egypt, Asia Minor, and Mesopotamia. It would appear that

Thothmes III. had a fleet on the Euphrates, and in an action which took place with the Assyrians, he defeated and chased the enemy for the distance of an Egyptian *atur*, supposed to be equal to the Greek *skoinos*, or single towing of a boat. Eighty men, thirty women, 606 slaves, were captured on the occasion, and the monarch, who had advanced beyond Ninii or Nineveh, returned to that city. The king set up a tablet on the occasion which recorded, like a trophy, his victories, and at the same time marked like a boundary stone the limits of his empire. The tribute received consisted of 513 slaves, 260 horses, gold to the amount of forty-five pounds, and gold vases, the work of the Tahai. These great craters or goblets, often mentioned in Egyptian annals, and seen on the monuments, were of large size, with handles in shape of animals or the human figure, and with flowers or tall stems running round the tops. They were inlaid with cloisonné-work, not enamel, of stone of lapis lazuli, glass, and other precious stones, or their imitations. They were as celebrated at this period as the vases of Sidon were at a later date; and the Tahai, as already mentioned, were situated to the North of Palestine.

Besides the vases, chariots, which the Egyptians required for the purposes of war, 564 head of cattle and 5323 goats, incense, products and fruit came from the same land to Egypt. It will be remarked that neither the camel nor the sheep is enumerated among the herds brought by the Egyptians. The zebu or the humped buffalo, and the horse, are principally mentioned; asses came but seldom, and there were rarer animals, offered as curiosities to the Egyptian monarchs to stock their parks. Some unimportant contributions are mentioned from the land of Ermen or Armenia; they are principally ducks, for domestic fowl had not yet left the jungles of India. Besides the tribute of Naharaina or Mesopotamia, the prince or king of Senkara or Singura, brought in the same year lapis lazuli, a substance much prized and often mentioned in the Egyptian inscriptions. Some of this came from Babalu or Babylon. An artificial imitation of blue color was often moulded into a small shape, and specimens exactly alike as to material, have been found on the banks of the Euphrates and the Nile. The chief of Singara offered in that year the head of a ram of that substance. It weighed fifteen Egyptian ounces or 2100 grs. troy. The tribute of another country, supposed to be the Khita, but possibly the Rutennu, came in the same year to the king on his return from the campaign in Mesopotamia. It consisted of 301 pounds of silver in eight rings, a great block of some peculiar stone, and the usual chariots. It has been already seen how Hasheps, the sister of the king, had explored for the first time the land of Arabia; and in this same year Punt or Arabia supplied 1685 quantities, called *haks*, of spices; while Kush or Ethiopia sent 134 slaves and 419 head of cattle, beside boat loads of ivory, ebony, panther skins, and other products. Uaua also contributed a tribute of the like kind. In the thirty-fourth year of his reign the king entered on his ninth expedition, and attacked the land of Tahai. He took three fortresses, one of which, Anaukasa, has been already mentioned, besides prisoners, women, and children, forty horses, chariots, above fifty pounds of gold in rings and vases, and 153 pounds of silver, 326 head of cattle, 130 goats, and seventy asses, besides various kinds of wools, and the poles of a tent. Asses formed part of the tribute of these people. The annual tribute of the Rutennu or Syrians in the same year, was thirty-four chariots, 704 slaves, also fifty-four pounds of gold, all sorts of gems, copper or iron *baa*, lead, various stones, felspar, 530 head of cattle, eighty-four asses, quantities of dates, balsam, wine. Each of the stations, or probably the garrisoned posts of the country, was provided with all necessary things for its maintenance, while boats or galleys from it traversed the sea, bringing with them the logs of the different kinds of wood so imperatively required for the treeless valley of the Nile. In the same year the chief or prince, Asi, also brought a tribute of copper, lead, lapis lazuli, while Kush or Ethiopia, brought its cattle, 275 in number, ivory and ebony, and the Uauat 254 pounds of gold and ten slaves, for as a general rule the South was richer than the North in gold. In the thirty-fifth year of his reign the king began his tenth campaign. Unfortunately the details are much mutilated on the monuments, but it appears that a battle of considerable importance was fought in Naharaina, where an army had been concentrated to resist the progress of the Egyptians. They are said to have been defeated and cut in pieces, falling on one another in their flight, and the land was spoiled again. Chariots, armor, and bows were the principal things taken; some of the bows came from the Kharubu, possibly Aleppo; for it was thence at a later period that the Pharaohs obtained the delicious wine of Syria. The battle took place at a spot called Arana. In the same year came other tribute from Ethiopia. Fragments only remain of the tributes of his thirty-seven years, when Kharu and Kush brought their usual quota of slaves and cattle. In the next year, the thirty-eighth, Thothmes began a new campaign, the thirteenth of his expeditions: he sacked the country of Anaukasa, which must have revolted from his yoke. The tributes and spoils were of the same nature as those previously detailed; captives, horses, chariots and slaves, collar of gold, vases, some of the class called by the Greeks *rhyton*, and which could not be laid on the table till the contents were drank out. These were in shape of the head of a lion or goat, and weighed 2821 pounds of gold. Conserves or balsam, cattle, forty-six asses and one deer, tables of cedar and ivory, fragrants and other woods, were contributed by the different cities, as also a galley, the work of Remennu or Armenia, fruit of Tahai or Northern Phœnicia, metals from the Asi, apparently a country of mines and rich in the products of the lower metals, are mentioned. From the land of Ameresk or Elasi, the chief sent male and female slaves, vases, thirty-five logs of cedar wood, showing that it was seated in the highlands of Armenia. Punt or Arabia contributed its gums and spices, obtained by the negroes, and Kush sent 111 slaves, 306 head of cattle, while Uauat sent slaves, cattle, and other products. Next year, the thirty-ninth, was the fourteenth campaign, and in this the king attacked the Shasu, but it does not appear if successfully, and a tribute was brought by the Rutennu or Syrians, the most remarkable portion of which was 1497 pounds of silver, and the usual plate or gold and silver vases of the Tahai, which had also sent some tribute of corn and wine in the same year. Possibly to the fortieth year is to be referred contributions of the Asi, which sent ivory as well as metals. In the forty-first year the king again attacked Aranta and Tunep, and received the usual tribute from the lands of the Rutennu and the Khita. The operations of this or the next year were directed against the fort of Aranatu and the fortresses of Kanana. He approached the land of Tunep, destroyed the fort, took the corn, and laid waste the groves. He also seems to have had another expedition against Kadesh, and to have fought the people of Naharaina, and in the battle which ensued a great deal of spoil was taken. In the unfortunately fragmentary texts which follow, the Tanai or Danai are mentioned, as also vases of the Kefa or Phœnicia, and the usual tributes of Kush or Ethiopia. The victories of the monarch were supposed to be due to the interposition, the gift, or the oracular responses of the god Amen, and the monarch in gratitude offered sacrifices to the god and offerings of various kinds. He made workshops for the slaves of the temple, and appointed negro doorkeepers, and gave four milch cows, some from the land of Tahai, to fill the golden milk-pails which supplied the services of the god. The three fortresses of the Rutennu, named Anaukasa, Iunamaa, and Hurantalu, were charged with supplying other food. The lake of the temple was provided with geese, and two offered at sunset daily. The four obelisks placed at the pylons or doors of the temple had also a kind of sacrifice or offering appointed to them, probably as types of the god Amen. Each obelisk had twenty-five rations of bread, and one draught or pint of beer.

The sacred statues placed at the threshold or jambs of the door, had also offerings appointed to their worship. To the images he also gave sacred vestments. The meadow was renewed, and rich and varied offerings given to the god, and processions of the statues of the king and of the god were instituted. The captives that were taken in these wars, reduced to slavery, were employed on the public works like convicts of the present day. They are represented on the walls of a tomb at Thebes in such a manner that it depicts vividly to the eye the unjust and cruel slavery to which the people of Israel had been reduced by the Pharaoh who knew not Joseph. There are the brick makers, the drawers of water, the bearers of the heavy burdens, and the severe taskmasters of the land of bondage, while their Asiatic countenances resemble those of the Semitic, and especially the Hebrew race.

There are several monuments which supplement

the annals of the reign. The most remarkable is that of Rekhmara, an officer of high rank of the reign. There is the tribute of the Rutennu, who, besides the rich plate, the gold and silver vases, jars of wine, bring chariots, arms, snow-white steeds, and bay horses, the cinnamon-colored bear known as the Ursus Syriacus, found in the ranges of the Taurus, and a young Asiatic elephant, colored red, besides tusks of the same animal. As the elephant is not found nearer than India, and about eight centuries later, although brought as tribute to Shalmaneser, was not well known to the Assyrians, who represented it with the ears of a horse, it is evident that the Ruten extended their rule to the very confines of India. The tribute of Kefa or Phœnicia, and its dependent colonies "in the midst of the great basin or sea," consisted of gold and silver in rings, and vases of the shapes already described; but it is startling to find in the tribute a gold vase in shape of the head of a cock; an evident mistake of the modern artist for the eagle's head with raised feathers, as seen on the monuments of Assyria. Jewels, plates of gold, and ivory, are brought by this highly civilized people, whose short tunic round the loins, of many colors, resembles the Egyptians, but whose pointed shoes on the feet are those of the Etruscan *larths* or lords. Their hair is in front twisted into a kind of *brutus* or curl, and falls long down their backs behind. The races of the South appear probably as the natives of the land Uauat or distant countries, and of Kush or Ethiopia. The tributes of those nearest to Egypt, probably the Uauat, just beyond the boundaries of Assouan, are obelisks of red syenite, gold, silver, and jewels, ivory, panther skins, and the same animal, logs of ebony, the cynocephalus, and another ape, the ibex, but of smaller size, the eggs and feathers of the ostrich, and rare trees. The other races of Kush or Ethiopia bring the same, but in addition, red jasper, *hamka*, and the amazon stone or emerald, *kasem*. The animals are also of the same species, larger and smaller apes, but there are also the bloodhounds or the dogs that hunted men, mentioned at a later period as sent by Queen Candace. Two different kinds of long-horned-oxen also appear in droves; one variety has the horns turned down; of these oxen some are white, and others red. The herds of Ethiopia have been mentioned in the statistical tablet or annals of Thothmes, and the tomb of Rekhmara is a series of vignettes or pictorial comments on the events there described. Other monuments record some of the actions of Thothmes, the obelisk of the Atmeidan at Constantinople the conquest of Mesopotamia.

There is however one monument which describes in poetical language the exploits and extent of the dominions of Thothmes. It speaks in the name of Ammon, and declares that the god has let the king extend his rule to the poles of heaven and limits of the earth. Thothmes, it states, had navigated the sea and the great rivers of Mesopotamia, had conquered the Aamu or Asiatics, and taken Kadesh Taha or Northern Syria, Taneter or Northern Arabia the seats of the Maten or Asia Minor, the Tahennu or Libyans, the Isles of Tena or the Danai, in the Mediterranean, probably those of the Archipelago, Kenus or Nubia, Remen or Armenia, Kefa or Phœnicia, the country of Asi, perhaps the original name of Asia, the Isles of the Utena, and that already at the time of the sixth dynasty. "I have let thee smite," it says, "the land of Taha or Northern Syria; I have let them see thy majesty; as the lord of sunbeams, thou shinest in their faces like my image. I have let thee," it adds in another passage, "smite the East; thou hast marched in the confines of the land of Taneter; it sees thy majesty like a comet, which warms by its fire and throws forth its vapor." In similar strains the great conqueror is compared to the bull, the lion, the crocodile, and the hawk, all used in the hieroglyphs to indicate the idea of a king and a hero. It will be seen that the exploits of Thothmes correspond to those of Sesostris, whose armies and victories are supposed to embrace the world as known to the ancients, and to have penetrated to the North of Greece, and almost to Central Europe.

The last monument of this important reign is that of Amenemheb, one of the generals of that day. He had fought in the land of Kabu, and taken three prisoners, and as many in Mesopotamia; thirteen others he had taken in the land of Van, which lay to the West of Kharubu or Aleppo, besides seventy asses, and other prisoners at the well-known site of Karakamasha or Carchemish. In his first campaign against Kadesh he had made two officers of the enemy prisoners, and killed in combat an enemy in the land of Tachisi, and captured three more prisoners. The king, who appears to have liberally rewarded his great captain, to whom the success of his arms was due, with a munificence worthy of so great a sovereign, bestowed upon Amenemheb collars, bracelets, and buckles of gold, chains, and silver rings, besides the decorations of flies and lions, which were, like the modern cross, an honorable distinction to mark the person of the monarch or the services of his officers. Amenemheb had accompanied the king to the land of Nii, apparently India or its confines, and was there present at the hunt of 120 elephants, which the king chased for their ivory. The largest or rogue elephant of the herd rushed at the monarch, and the king was saved by Amenemheb, who cut off its trunk and captured the beast alive. Another of the actions of this officer was crossing the waters at the spot known as the Two Rocks, situated in Syria or Mesopotamia. He was also present at a battle before Kadesh, so often attacked by Egypt. The king of Kadesh started a wild mare to run against the king, and she got amongst the troops or division of Amenemheb; but this valiant officer followed her a foot, ripped her up, and cut off the tail, which he presented to the king. Present at the second siege of Kadesh, he breached the walls and led the forlorn hope, taking two more prisoners on the occasion. He appears to have afterwards been captain of the royal barge at Thebes.

The empire extended in the South to the Karu or Kalu, apparently the Gallas and Abyssinia; and a series of temples and monuments at Amada, Corte, Talmis, Pselcis, Semneh, and Koumme, bear his name. Ethiopia or the Soudan was governed by Nahi, a royal son or "a prince of Kush," who ruled the country in the name of the king, and to whom was no doubt due the regular remission of the tribute. At Abu or Elephantine, a temple to Khnum was constructed, and an obelisk from it is at Sion House. At Ombos, Esneh or Latopolis, Eileithyia, and Hermonthis, Thothmes erected also temples, but all of them except a few stones have disappeared. The capital of the dynasty, however, "Thebes with its hundred gates," was most favored by the monarch. In the Karnak quarter he built a small temple to Ptah, and the so-called granite sanctuary. The tombs in Libyan range, behind Gournah, and the El-Assasif are full of scenes of the reign of Thothmes. Two great obelisks of 108 cubits high, with gilded tops, are recorded in these sepulchres, as also the vast sum of 36,692 tens of gold. At Memphis and Heliopolis the name of Thothmes shows that these cities had not been neglected. A tablet of the forty-seventh year of his reign records that he had surrounded the temple of the god Ra or the Sun, at An, or the biblical On, as the city was called, with a wall, while the magnificent obelisks of Alexandria and Rome with his name seem to have come from that city. At the Sarabit-el-Khadim, in the Arabian peninsula, besides the tablet of the sixteenth year of his reign with his sister, one of the twenty-fifth year of his sole dominion, an officer records that he had come at the head of his troops to convey that which was agreeable to the monarch, the products of the lands of the gods of *mafka*, turquoise or copper. A fragment of a papyrus in the British Museum has the account of an historical incident not elsewhere found. It records the betrayal of a fortress of the Juima or people of the sea by an Egyptian officer in their confidence. The stratagem by which the place was taken recalls to mind the story of Ali Baba rather than a military event. Two hundred men were put with cords and yokes into jars. Thus introduced into the city, they bound the garrison with bonds, and handed the town over to Thothmes. As all the other compositions on the same papyrus are works of imagination, this may after all not be an historical event. The Aperu, supposed by some to be the Hebrews, are mentioned amongst the other nations conquered by Thothmes.

On the 30th of the month Phamenoth, in the fifty-fourth year of his reign, Thothmes died. From the youthful age at which he had been placed upon the throne it is not probable that his life exceeded sixty years, enough for one so glorious and so active, and who has left so indelible a streak in the history of the world. His wife bore the same name as his sister; she was probably of the family, but it is uncertain if she was the mother of his successor.

Although some incline to the idea that the Exodus took place about this reign, as the more prevalent idea is that it happened at the close of the next dynasty, it is merely necessary to point here to that supposition, reserving its consideration to that part of the narrative.

His successor, Amenhetp II., ascended his throne surrounded by difficulties. It is always more difficult to retain than to acquire foreign conquests. The Asiatics threw off the yoke of Egypt, and Amenhetp had to march like his predecessor to the plains of Mesopotamia. There he made eighteen Asiatic prisoners, and captured himself nineteen head of cattle. Subsequently the monarch took the city of Nineveh, the present Kouyunjik, and a city named Akerti or Akourit. A tablet at the temple of Amada, dedicated to the gods Harmachis and Amon, records some of the exploits of Amenhetp. It states that he had killed with his mace seven kings in the town of Takhisa, and slung them before his war galley. Six of these kings and their hands were hanged before the ramparts of Thebes. The other king or chief was sent down the river to Nubia, and hanged on the walls of Napata, as an example to the negroes, ever too ready to revolt. At Thebes, amongst his prisoners, recur the names of Nubia, the Shasu or Arabs, and Phœnicians, which he had to reconquer. His reign was short, but its exact duration is uncertain. Tablets of the fourth and seventh year of his reign are found at the Sarabit-el-Khadim.

His successor, Thothmes IV., is chiefly known in connection with the great Sphinx at Gizeh, one of the marvels of the old world. It is by no means certain that he cut this monument out of the solid rock, for it appears from the chapel in its neighborhood, and an inscription already cited in the fourth dynasty, to have been a work of a more remote antiquity. In his first year Thothmes set up a votive tablet of fourteen feet high between the forepaws of this colossal work, which measures more than 180 feet in length. The tablet records the merits of the king in embellishing Heliopolis and Memphis. The Sphinx represented Harmachis or the Sun on the horizon, and the king refers his ascension of the throne to the favor of that god. It has been remarked that the great devotion of Thothmes to the worship of Ra or the Sun, shown here and elsewhere, foreshadowed the religious revolution which took place at the close of the reign of his successor. The triumphs of his reign consisted of some easy conquests, in the South, of negro tribes, recorded on a tablet of the seventh year of his reign in the island of Konosso.

Thothmes also reigned but a short time, and was succeeded by Amenhetp III., or Amenophis, considered by the Greek epitomists to be Memnon, the son of Heos or Aurora, who appeared at the head of his dusky warriors at the Trojan War, on the slender foundation of his statue at Thebes giving out musical sounds at sunrise. The tablets sculptured on the rocks at the quarries of Tourah, near the ancient Memphis, dated in the first and second year of his reign, announce that he had re-opened them for the reparation of the temples of the North and South. The first historical inscription of his reign is the account of some triumphs over the negroes in his fifth year, inscribed on a tablet engraved on the rocks in the neighborhood of Philæ, and designated one of his first campaigns. A tablet from Samneh mentions the rapid passage which the king had made on the Upper Nile in a day and an hour, where he sailed or rowed fifty-two atours, an unknown distance, no doubt of considerable length, extending from the station of Baka, and reaching to Atarii or Adulis. In this great razzia the king had taken a great number of prisoners of war or rather slaves, amounting to 150 negroes, 110 boys, 250 negresses, 55 judges, 175 of their children, 740 in all, besides the usual trophies of 312 hands of the dead enemy, making a total of 1052 head of negroes, killed and captured in this one expedition. It is remarkable to find the negroes counted like cattle, by "heads" instead of "persons," as the Egyptians are, and that they were not ruled by kings or chiefs, but by "judges," an institution subsequently adopted by the Hebrews after the Exodus. There is no trace of such a form of government in Egypt, but it may have been the result of a theocratic rule prevailing at the time amongst the inhabitants of Kush. It is probable that the queen Tii was about this time married to the monarch. Her origin was evidently foreign, for she is represented as pink or flesh-colored, the tint of the Japhetic races on the monuments. The scarabaei which record their marriage state that her father's name was Iuaa, and her mother's Tuaa. This strange and probably foreign woman exerted at a later period a marked influence on the politics of Egypt. The scarabæi issued in his tenth year mention that from the first to the tenth year he had killed with his own arrows 110 fierce lions, a passion for the chase like Nimrod, or for the battue like that of an Assyrian monarch or Roman gladiator. At a later period another monarch of Egypt was seen giving battle to these lords of the desert, or entering the battle-field accompanied by his faithful lion. Some scarabæi dated in his eleventh year, foreshadow the religious revolution which was impending. On the first of the month Athyr of that year he had constructed a great lake or basin, 3000 cubits long and 600 cubits broad, or about 5000 feet by 1000 feet, English measure. On the 16th of the month he celebrated a festival, and brought into it the boat of the solar disk, called *Atennefru*, "the most lovely disk." This worship of the sun's orb or disk was not unknown in Egypt, and was allied with that of Ra. In the Aten may perhaps be recognized the solar disk or orb specially worshipped by the Ethiopians, and the mother of Amenophis was of that race. In it some have seen the Hebrew Adonai or "Lord," and the Syrian Adonis. To this new form of worship, allied with that of the sun, Amenophis inclined, but it was necessary to introduce it by degrees, and at the close of his reign the attempt to change the capital and religion of the country was unsuccessfully made.

In the same year there is a tablet recording certain endowments of the temple of Karnak, and invoking curses on all daring to disturb the provisions of its gift, or employ the slaves on other work than the service of the temple. While Ethiopia continued to be governed by a royal prince or viceroy, who was named at this time Merimes, the frontiers of Egypt continued to reach to the land of Mesopotamia. Asiatic and negro tributaries are seen in the tombs of Thebes prostrating themselves in his presence and offering the accustomed tribute of ivory, ostrich feathers, panther skins, baskets of gems, and metals; while at the temple of Soleb the lands of the North, Naharaina or Mesopotamia, Singara, Pattana or Padan-Aram, and Assur or *Assyria* are recorded amongst his conquests or possessions. His chief exploits were, however, over the Ethiopians, and his dominion reached to Karu or Kalu, perhaps Coloe, or Gallas in the South. The numerous Nigritic names recorded on his monuments show that the South particularly attracted his attention.

A monument of the thirtieth year of his reign represents him receiving the account of a great harvest from the store-keepers of Upper and Lower Egypt. This monarch also renewed the construction of the Sarbit-el-Khadim in the peninsula of Sinai, and tablets with his name dated in his thirty-fifth and thirty-sixth years, have been found on the site, the last of those of the eighteenth dynasty. Amenophis was a great builder of palaces and temples; and the temple of Amon-Ra at Luxor, that of Khnum at Elephantine, and of Soleb in Nubia, besides the two colossal statues

Khuenaten adoring the Sun's disk.

which he placed before the palace of Luxor, representing him seated on his throne, attest his devotion to architecture and sculpture. The Northern colossus, the upper part of which was broken by an earthquake B.C. 27, was the so-called vocal Memnon. Restored by the Roman emperor Severus about A.D. 160, it spoke no more to the rising beams of morning. Amenophis must lie under the reproach of having been too much under female influence, but the empire was still maintained in its integrity. His son, Amenhetp IV., who had been appointed in the lifetime of his father, became an heretical fanatic of the worst sort. He carried the worship of the "disk," or Aten, to its extreme limits, and persecuted all other forms of deities except those of the purely solar gods. In this he appears to have been principally guided by his mother, the queen Tii, and the eunuchs and other officers of his court. The disk itself was represented shedding rays of light which often terminated in hands, and in the hymns addressed to it in the tombs, is considered to be the same as Amon-Ra, the creative power of the deity and the creator and ruler of time. Amenhetp endeavored to remove the capital to Alabastron, the modern Tel-el-Amarna, and the tablets and inscriptions there dated in the sixth year of his reign, record his homage to the disk. Not only are the scenes represented peculiar—the king is seen showering on his court donations of various kinds from a window of the palace, while the types, features, and the abject prostration of his court, and unusual freedom of art, show the introduction of a foreign element into the annals of the country. His power extended over Egypt and part of Asia. At Silsilis is recorded the extraction of an obelisk for the god Harmachis; a sanctuary he had raised at Thebes was pulled down by his successor to construct a gateway. The usual tributes came from the Kharu or Khalu of the North, the people of the East, the isles of the Mediterranean, and Kush, while Asiatic and negro soldiers filled the ranks of his army. His reign did not extend for long time, and he had no male issue, but two daughters, whom he associated with him in the empire, in order to succeed him.

It would appear that Khuenaten, the name substituted in the latter days of Amenophis IV., for his original appellation, was succeeded after a short reign by another monarch, who had married a queen bearing the name of Atenmerit. They might have flourished for a short time only, as the next monarch Ai, or Aui, had held under Amenophis IV. the rank of fan-bearer at the king's right hand, and groom of the royal stud. He played an important part during the reign of Khuenaten. His name is found on the blocks of the pylon of Horus, and tablets of his first and fourth year are known of officers of his court, but the name of Amen is not erased on these, and those of the usual deities appear. Yet he was an object of hatred to his successors, and the avenging chisel has mutilated his name and features in his tomb, showing evidently that it was violated, had he indeed been buried there. His tomb was in the western valley, and not finished.

His successor was Tutankhamen, whose name was given to him in honor of the Theban god. It may perhaps be conjectured that this monarch did not immediately succeed, but it is clear that his place in the dynasty is at its close. It is, however, remarkable that Kush or Ethiopia continued in his reign to be administered by Hui and Amenhetp, the same princes who are mentioned as governors in the reign of Amenophis III. A tomb at Thebes represents the tributes of the Rutennu or Syrians; they bring as tributes vases of silver, gold, lapis lazuli, turquoise, and all the precious stones of the country, and the usual presents of horses and chariots. The prince of Ethiopia, Hui, sent up a great embassy of negroes, both black and copper-colored, accompanied by their queen drawn in a bullock car. Besides the oxen, horses, and other animals, the negroes bring many objects which show a high refinement, and prove the influence of Egyptian civilization and their capacity for improvement. At a later period it will be seen that they brought chairs and other articles of furniture as offerings to Egypt. The reigns of the monarchs who succeeded Amenophis III. up to this period, are supposed to have lasted thirty-four years, and their names do not appear in the royal lists of Abydos, either that they were considered usurpers, or that chronologically the duration of their power was reckoned under their predecessors and successors on the throne.

The last monarch of this dynasty was Haremhebi, or *Horus*, of the lists of Manetho. No remarkably glorious event distinguished his reign. Monuments are known dated in the seventh year of his reign. Piety or his beholding the gods, according to the Greek epitomists, was his characteristic; but he made one campaign at least against the Ethiopians. In the sculptures of Silsilis are seen his exploits against that people, and the legends which accompany the representation of his triumphal march in a palanquin, call him "The Lion of Kush." "His bow," they add, " is in his hand, like Mentu lord of Thebes, the powerful and glorious king, leading captive the chiefs of the isle Kush. He returns thence with the spoils he has captured as his father Amon ordered him." These consisted of silver and gold, ivory and ebony. The chant of the negroes as they are led along is, "Incline thy face, oh king of Egypt, Sun of Barbarians, great is thy name in Kush, and thy war-cries in its places; thy valor, oh good king, has defeated the nations. Pharaoh is my sun!" Horus destroyed the edifices of the heretic monarchs at Thebes, and built with the stones the fourth gateway of the temple at Karnak, in honor of Amon, re-established in his pristine glory. The name of the god which had been cut out of the monuments of the country was also reinserted in his reign.

The manner in which the nineteenth dynasty succeeded the eighteenth is unknown, probably owing to Horus not having any family, as although the name of his wife Mutsnatem occurs on the monuments, no prince or other member of his family is mentioned. The first monarch of the dynasty was Rameses or Ramses I., and he is supposed to have been connected with marriage with the previous family. Perhaps the wife of Horus survived that monarch, for she is represented on the monument under the form of a female sphinx, showing that she exercised sovereignty in her sole person, and Ramses may have married either the widow of his predecessor or her daughter, and no queen of this monarch is known. Little is known of the reign of Rameses. A tablet of the Wady Halfa in Nubia, dated in the second year of his reign, records that he constructed a prison full of slaves, whom he had taken prisoners in war, for the god Khem or Amen Horus. From the treaty of his successor, Rameses II., it appears that he had made a campaign against the Khita in Northern Syria, and made a treaty with Separuru or Sapor, the king who at that time ruled over the Hittites. The details are however unknown. The tomb of Rameses is in the Biban-el-Molook at Thebes, and the paintings represent him adoring the usual sepulchral deities, especially Tum or the setting sun, lord of Heliopolis, and demiurgos or creator of beings, who promises the sun to come forth like the sun in heaven, and be like that luminary. Rameses had no time to recover the lost power and territories of Egypt, and the task devolved on his son and successor Seti I. The first year of this monarch represents him in arms against the Asiatics, and his victories almost equal those of the kings of the eighteenth dynasty. His battles are sculptured on the outer walls of the temple of Amon at Karnak, in a series of pictures representing his successive campaigns. In the first of these the monarch is in the country of the Remenen or Armenia; the chiefs appear in homage before him, cutting down their woods to construct a fleet on the river. This country is stated to be connected with the Ruten, the Assyria or Northern Syria. In the second of these pictures Seti mounted in his chariot attacked the Shasu or Arabs. These invaders of Egypt, who had made themselves masters of the country just prior to the eighteenth dynasty, had evidently again invaded the Eastern frontier, for the accompanying Egyptian inscriptions state that in his first year Sethos "had attacked the hostile Shasu, who inhabit the town of Pithom, even to the land of Kanana or 'Canaan.' His majesty surprised them like a strong lion, and made a slaughter of them in their valley. They lay on the ground in their blood, so that none could escape his fury to tell his prowess to the people."

In the third picture Seti attacks the Rutennu, and later the fortress of Innumau, which had been formerly captured by Thothmes III., and its revenues bestowed on the temple of Amon. In the battle under its walls the chariots of the enemy were entirely routed. In this third picture the king enters the desert occupied by the Shasu, and changes the names of the fortresses taken in the march into Egyptian ones connected with his own, as if founded by him to maintain his conquests. The Kharu or Khalu, a maritime people, apparently on the coast of Syria, offer tribute and submission. On his return to Egypt his chariot is laden with the chiefs of the Ruten, whom he drags at its wheels like the legendary Sesostris, and this forms the subject of the fifth picture. In the last of the series he marches back by the desert of Uagi, Makatala or Migdol, and the City of the Lions, or Leontopolis, to the fort of Taru or Garu, the frontier town of Egypt, probably Heroopolis, if it is not Pithom, which has been at all times the frontier and key of Egypt. It is represented as placed on the left bank of the Nile, and the river is full of crocodiles, which at that time descended almost if not quite to the sea. Over the stream is a bridge, the earliest example in the monuments of this mode of traversing a river. The inscription states that the prophet, high-priests, and chiefs or governors of Upper and Lower Egypt, have come to make obeisance to the king on his victorious return from the land of the Ruten. "Thou hast returned," it says, "from the lands thou hast defeated, justified against thy enemies. The length of thy reign is like that of the sun in heaven; thou hast washed thy heart in the barbarians, and the sun has placed thy frontiers. The arms of the sun have protected thee, while thy mace fell on the heart of all the countries, and thy sword slaughtered their inhabitants." From Garu or Galu the monarch proceeded to Thebes, and descended from his war chariot at the gate of the temple of Amon. He was accompanied by the chiefs or princes of the Ruten; and in reply to his address the god says to him that Amon himself accorded the victories and the safe return to the metropolis. After his return the captives are represented led up in a long file to the Theban deities, Amon-Ra, the goddess Mut, and their son Khonsu, a lunar god. The prisoners ask favor or mercy of the king, and aver that they knew not Egypt, and that their forefathers had never trod upon its soil. Such at least is the declaration of the Rutennu. That of the Shasu or Arabs is not the same, but it is stated that they were conquered in the first year of the reign of Seti. In the accompanying list of prisoners, whose hieroglyphic names encircled in embattled ovals or enclosures, fifty-nine in number, are placed on the adjacent wall, are mentioned among the Northern countries the Hanebu, the supposed Javans Iones, or Ionians, as the Greeks were always called by the Egyptians, the Eastern Shepherds, the Khita or Hittites, Naharaina or Mesopotamia, the Ruten just cited, the Punt or Arabs of Southern Arabia, the Shasu or Hyk-shos, and many towns of Central Asia, besides several appellations of Kushite tribes of Nubia and Abyssinia. It is in this reign that the Khita first appears in history, and Seti attacked the town of Kadesh, said to be part of the land of Amor or the Amorites, but under the jurisdiction of the Khita. It is situated in an island in the midst of the Arunata or Orontes, and is supposed to be the modern Hums or ancient Edessa. These people, like the Hyk-shos, were attached to the worship of the god Seti or Seth, known to the Egyptians as Typhon or the Satan. The local goddess of Kadesh was Anata or Anaitis, the Bellona or goddess of war of the land of Canaan, and she appears armed with spear and shield when introduced into the worship of Egypt. In Canaan and the neighboring countries, Bar or Baal, the local god of Tyre prevailed, and his worship was attended to by that of Astaruta, the Ashtaroth or Astarte of the Scriptures, to whom was built a temple at Memphis. Reshpu, or Reseph, another Semitic deity, mentioned in the Phœnician inscriptions as Reseph-Mical, also was introduced about the same period into Egyptian temples. He too armed with a spear, appears to have been a god of war. Seti perhaps commenced the canal which joined the Nile with the Red Sea. It started from Bubastis and entered the Bitter Lakes. He occupied with his forces Tyre, Avathus, and Bethanath. In Canaan he built new fortresses to hold the countries. Sethos also came into conflict with the Tahennu or Libyans. The

Western neighbors of Egypt had already been attacked by Thothmes and Amenophis, probably in return of the incursions which they were continually making on the exposed Western frontier of Egypt. They were a branch, if not identical with the Tamahu, and were distinguished by having their hair shaved and plaited into a lock at the right side of the head, while two ostrich feathers were placed on the top of the crown. For dress they wore a long cloak or tunic, open in front, and for arms they had only bows and arrows. It would appear that they inhabited the Atlas range, and were perhaps Troglodytes; for in the inscription which accompanies the scene, representing Seti in his chariot defeating their host, it is stated that "he stood in the pass of the annihilated bearing bows, watching in their caves like wolves lying in wait for his majesty." This description corresponds with the condition of the Kabyles and other Arab tribes, who even in recent times when conquered in the field, have fled for protection to the caverns of the Atlas range. But the victories of Seti were only a portion of the alternate vicissitudes of Egypt, exposed on the West to the incursions of the barbarians of Western Asia, whose only curb was the intervening desert.

His conquests of the South are mentioned at Karnak, and Kush or Ethiopia, was governed by the royal prince or viceroy, Amenemapet. Evidences of his dominion are found at Sesebi; at Rhedesieh or *Contra Pselcis*, opposite the town of *Apollinopolis Magna* or Edfu. Seti constructed a sanctuary for the local gods, and made a tank or well for the supply of the miners who crossed the desert to go to the ancient gold mines, but many of whom perished for want of water on the way. In this he is said to have but to say the word, and the water would leap out of the living rock; a metaphor indeed in his case, but an expression that forcibly calls to mind the miraculous action of Moses in the desert. At Beni-el-Hassan, or the Speos Artemidos, he made a small rock temple to the goddess Sekhet, the wife of Ptah and the Nemesis of the enemies of Egypt. A stelé at Silsilis records his victories over the Kharu or Syrians, and Kush or Ethiopia, and another dated in the ninth year of his reign at Assouan, the monuments he had made. At Sesebi his dominion is said to have reached "on the South the arms of the winds, and on the North the Great Sea." The Flaminian obelisk at Rome, at present in the Piazza del Popolo, and removed from Egypt to Rome to ornament the Circus Maximus by Augustus B.C. 19, was originally placed by Seti at Heliopolis. His tomb in the Biban-el-Meluk, discovered by the traveller Belzoni, and which contained his alabaster sarcophagus, now in the Sloane Museum of London, was ornamented with great care, and depicted the passage of the sun through the hours of the night. The name of Seti has often experienced injury from a subsequent religious revolution, the name of the god Set having been effaced by the chisel, and that of Osiris substituted in its place. The fifty-one years attributed to his reign by the epitomists are not confirmed by the monuments.

Seti was succeeded by Rameses II., one of the most remarkable of Egyptian kings for his personal exploits, the magnificence of his monuments, and the duration of his reign. From his popular appellation, Sestesura, and its varieties, he was known to the Greeks as Sesostris, and the events and conquests of other monarchs added to his own. He ascended the throne a mere youth, having apparently attained less than ten years. His first campaigns were directed against the people of Kush or Ethiopia. Some of the later campaigns are apparently the subject of the sculptures of the passage leading to the temple at Beitoualli in Nubia. These represent the prince Amenhèrsemif introducing, into the presence of Rameses, Amenemapt, prince-viceroy of Ethiopia, accompanied by the tributaries and tributes of that country, lions, gazelles, oxen, panthers, the camelopard, and the ostrich, and the defeat of the negroes by Rameses in person, attended by his sons, Amenhèrsemif and Shaæmuas. The great event of the reign of Rameses, was the campaign against the Khita in his fifth year. It commenced on the ninth of the month Epiphi, and is represented or described in the temples of Luxor, Abusimbel, Beitoualli, and the Ramesseum, as well as on a papyrus in the British Museum, known as the Sallier Papyrus, in which the events are described in terms resembling an Epic poem, which has been called the Iliad of Egypt. Rameses marched against the confederation of Central Asia, headed by the king of the Khita and his allies, comprising the people of Carchemish, the Khirubu or Chalybes, the Maouna or Ilion. The king desired to know the position of the enemy, as the Egyptian army ascended the Arunata or Orontes and approached Kadesh. Two spies of the Rubu or Arabs came and informed the monarch that the king of the Khita, frightened at the approach of the Egyptian host, had marched to the South, and were drawn up in the land of the Khirubu. But the forces of the Khita were concentrated to the Northwest of Kadesh. The advanced guard of the king seized however the two spies, and these, bastinadoed by the orders of the king, confessed that they had been sent to reconnoitre the Egyptians, and that the allied armies lay behind Kadesh on the Northwest, watching their enemies, and waiting for an opportunity to attack Rameses. The king assembled his generals, reprimanded them for their neglect, and told them that instead of lying to the South, the army of the Khita was posted on the North of Kadesh, and about to attack them in the rear. The generals admitted the fault of their manœuvres, and an officer was despatched towards the main army, already on the march to the South, and uncovering by its movement the position of the king. In the meantime the king of the Khita and his allies marched to the South of Kadesh, and before the Egyptian host could retrace their steps the staff of Rameses was dispersed, and the Egyptian monarch found himself surrounded with the chariots of the allied forces. The monuments describe Rameses at this moment as seizing his arms, encouraging his dismayed charioteer, marching alone to attack the Khita, and breaking their ranks. The victory rested with the Egyptians; the Khita killed and wounded comprised Grabatusa, the charioteer of the king of the Khita, Rabsuna, the general of the troops, Tarakennas, the general of the cavalry, Khirapusar, scribe or secretary; Matsurama, the brother of the king of the Khita, and the king of the Khirubu, half-drowned in the waters of the Orontes. The king of the Khita descended from his chariot and humbly entreated peace from Rameses. In the poem of Pentaur the king is described "as all alone, no other with him; when he looked behind him he found himself encircled with 2500 chariots obstructing his way, and all the men of the vile Khita and their numerous lands—there were three men on a chariot," the same number as the Hebrews in their Exodus. After an address to Amon, stating the counsels he had followed and the offerings he had given the god, and reiterating that he was in the midst of the 2500 chariots, he states then "they were overthrown before my steeds, not one of them found his hand to fight; their hearts sank within them, their hands dropped, they had no heart to grasp a spear; I made them sink into the water like crocodiles sink." On the fear of his charioteer Menna, who asks how they can hope to withstand the enemy,—"Courage! courage, my charioteer!" he exclaimed, "I will pierce them like a hawk. I will slay, cut them down, and throw them into the dust. What to thy heart are these Asiatics? Amon brings low those who know not God, his face is not white for millions of them." "Then," it adds towards the end, "the king of the vile Khita sent to do homage to the great name of the king Rameses. Thou art Ra, Harmachis; thou art Set, mighty in strength, son of Nut or the celestial ether, Baal himself. Thy terror is over the prostrate land of the Khita; thou hast broken the back of the Khita for ever and ever!" With all due allowance for poetic exaggeration and servile adulation, it is clear that Rameses had fallen into an ambuscade, and rescued himself by great daring and personal courage. The war did not however end with this battle, but continued till the ninth year of his reign.

In the eighth year of his reign Rameses took the fortress of Shaluma or Salem, supposed to be the ancient name of Jerusalem before its occupation by the Hebrews. In the same year Maram was taken, and Tapura of the land of Amaru or the Amorites, supposed to be Dabir, situated at the foot of Mount Tabor. Bethanath and Kamon were captured at the same time; as also Askaluna or Ascalon, then in possession of the Canaanites, not having yet fallen into the hands of the Philistines, which it subsequently did about the commencement of the twentieth dynasty. In his twenty-first year Rameses concluded an extraditionary treaty with Khitasar, the king of the Khita, at the fortress of Paramessu or Tanis, to which the two monarchs had gone for that purpose. In this treaty Khitasar refers to a previous one between his brother Mautmer and Seti, the father of Rameses. Khitasar it appears was the son of Maursar, and grandson of Separuru or Sapor, and his brother had been killed or assassinated. The treaty was a mutual agreement not to make incursions into each other's territories, nor aid and abet others in attacking one another. The Khita towns were placed under the protection of Sutech and Ashtaroth, those of Egypt under the Theban god Amon. Considerable difference of opinion has existed as to the names of the allies of the Khita, and some think that they are those of the Trojans and their confederates in Asia Minor; but in the temple at Abusimbel the Khita have a very Scythic character, with shaven hair, single lock from the crown, blue garments, and square worked shields, the so-called *gerrha*. It appears from a tablet at Abusimbel that Rameses married a daughter of the king of the Khita, and that she adopted the Egyptian name of Ra-maa-ur-neferu. Rameses had marched to this war along the coast of Palestine, and has left tablets at the Nahr-el-Kelb or Lycus, recording the passage of his forces to Northern Syria. At Beitoualli the Asiatic campaigns of the king appear to have been directed against the Amorites, the Canaanites, and his Libyan ones, and Kharu or Syrians, against the Tahennu and Mashuash or Maxyes. In this he is accompanied by his dog, named *Antæmnekht,* or "Anaitis in her strength." When seated on his throne the king is accompanied by a lion named *Smæmnekhtef*. All things in Egypt were named, not only favorite animals, but swords, sceptres, sticks and tools.

But the affairs of the South no less engaged the attention of Rameses. In his third year he had given orders for the excavation of a well at Redesieh or Contra Pselcis, to supply the miners and their asses, which crossed the desert to the land of Akaitau. In flattering language the deputation addressed the monarch; after explaining that the miners perished if no pools formed by the rainfall happened to exist. "If," said they, "thou formest a plan at night, it is realized in the day, and again if thou hast said to the waters, come out of the mountain, the celestial water comes according to your word." The king ordered the well to be made, and it was called the Well of Meriamoun-Rameses. The land of Akataui is probably Gebel Ollaki and the gold mines of that spot. The speech recalls to mind Moses, at the command of God, striking the rock of Horeb, and the water issuing from it. The great length of the reign of Rameses enabled him to construct many temples in Egypt and Nubia, on which he employed captives taken in war. For this purpose, as also to hold in check his numerous prisoners, he transported the negroes to the North, and the Asiatics to the South. At Gerf Hussein he founded the town of Paptah, and a temple dedicated to the Ptah of Rameses or Vulcan, the protector of the king. At Sebua, the town of Paamen, he built a similar town and temple, dedicated to the Amon of Rameses, and at Der, the city of Para, a temple dedicated to Ra.

The town of Abusimbel, called Paramessu, had a speos or cave temple, in which was represented the defeat of the Khita. On the Eastern side of Egypt he finished a great wall, commenced by his father Seti, from Pelusium to Heliopolis, as a bulwark against the Asiatics. It was on this line that it is supposed the king constructed the fortresses Pa-khatem-en-Garu, or citadel of Heroopolis, and Paramessu or Raamses, the two cities on which the Hebrews were employed, as mentioned in the book of Exodus: "And they built for Pharaoh treasure cities Pithom and Raamses."* Raamses was also the name of the land of Goshen, assigned to Jacob and his sons, and from this fact it has been generally supposed that the Exodus took place after the reign of Rameses, as the fort and land must have borne his name; and the political condition of Egypt with the conquests of Seti I. in Palestine, are adverse to the idea that it could have happened at a time when the arms of Egypt were triumphant in Syria and Palestine. In this case Rameses would be the monarch mentioned in Exodus i. 8: "Now there arose up a new king over Egypt who knew not Joseph, and he said unto his people, Behold the children of the people of Israel are more and mightier than we. Come on, let us deal wisely with them, lest they multiply and it come to pass that when there falleth out any war they join also unto our enemies, and fight against us, and get them up out of the land." This agrees with the great wall of Sesostris or Rameses, evidently made at

* Exodus i. 2.

a time when Egypt was not too able to resist the attacks on her Eastern frontier, and when a revolt of the Babylonian captives had resulted in Sesostris or Rameses conceding to them a city which they called Babylon, now the site of the modern Cairo. Such a state of affairs with the necessity of protecting the kingdom, already in its decline, by a "long wall," which forcibly recalls to mind that of China, made to shield that country from the Tartars, would have been favorable to the approaching Exodus. At the same time no country appears to have oscillated more in its political relations than Egypt, alternately planting its standards on the banks of the Orontes and the Tigris, or its very existence threatened by its powerful neighbors, and shut up between the desert of Sahara and the confines of Canaan. The works of Rameses are also found at An, the scriptural On, or Heliopolis, and San or Tanis. Tanis was, according to some, the same as Paramessu, and one of the principal towns of the Hyk-shos or Shepherds. On a tablet found at San, the king has recorded that a period of 400 years elapsed between his reign and that of Seti or Saites, one of the Shepherd kings. Important to the calculation of the chronology of the eighteenth dynasty, this tablet has also a bearing on the disputed question of the Exodus, and the period when it happened.

The oppression of the Israelites was one to which all hostile or conquered people were reduced. Thothmes, it has already been seen, treated his captives in the same manner, and made them, like convicts, build the crude edifices at Thebes. Rameses built the greater portion of the temple of Luxor, founded by Amenophis III., and added to it both obelisks and colossal statues; one of these obelisks is now in the Place de la Concorde, at Paris. The king also added considerably to the Karnak quarter of Thebes. At Gournah he enlarged and finished another temple built by his father Seti; and also the temple or edifice known to the ancients as the tomb of Osymandyas or the Ramesseum. The Greek authors state that here was sculptured the revolt of the Bactrians, who must have been represented by the Khita. On the ceiling of the Ramesseum, Rameses placed an astronomical projection of the heavens, probably intended to represent his

Brick of sun-dried clay and straw stamped with one of the names of Rameses II.

genethlion or horoscope. In the accompanying inscription, the star *Setp* or Sothis, the Dog-star, or Sirius is said to appear heliacally, or in the morning, just before sunrise at the commencement of the year; this is supposed to show that the calendar at that time had a fixed solar year of 365¼ days, and was not the wandering year of 365, which lost one day in four years, and by which year the Egyptians also reckoned. At the same palace he is seen celebrating the festival of Amon-Ra in his character of Khem, apparently the anniversary of the royal coronation, and carrying in procession the statues of his ancestors of Menes and the kings of the eleventh and eighteenth dynasties. His family was unprecedented in number, even in the annals of Egypt, and consisted of many sons and daughters.

The monuments have also recorded the names of three of his queens, but he must have married more in the course of his long life. One of his daughters, afterwards queen, named Bantanath, or "Daughter of Anaitis," was also a queen, but it is not known of whom she was the wife. Her name suggests a Semitic mother. Several of his sons died before him. Of these the last known from the monuments is Shæmuas, who for a long time was governor of Memphis, and who died in the fifty-fifth year of the reign of his father. His mummy was found in the Serapeum at Memphis, in one of the chambers of the mummies of the hill Apis, there buried; but the reason of his interment there is unknown.

In the reign of Thothmes, the name of the Aperiu, supposed to be the Hebrews, appears amongst the lists of people conquered by that monarch, which throws considerable doubt on their identity with the Hebrews. In the days of Rameses they still are mentioned as in a condition of servitude, quarrying and transporting stone for the great fortress of the city of Paramessu or Tanis, and they continue in the service of Egypt till a still later period of its history. The age attained by Rameses was probably very great, as his reign extended to upwards of sixty-six years. The rich tombs in the valley of Gournah, and the sepulchre of the monarch himself, attest the wealth and prosperity of the country. The country had, however, begun to decline; the kingdoms of Asia were more than a match for the power of Egypt, and although it was a golden age for literature and poetry, romance, letter-writing, and works of imagination flourished, sculpture sensibly declined, and the fatal influx of Asiatic blood and religions began to destroy the national religion. The Asiatic element evidently prevailed in the Delta, or modern Fayoum, and Rameses himself exhibits in his features the refined Asiatic, different from the Nigritic type of the kings of the eighteenth dynasty.

Menephtah, the successor of Rameses, was his thirteenth son, the others having already died at the time of the death of their aged parent. He had been appointed governor of Memphis at the decease of his brother Shæmuas, and his name and titles contain a mention of Ptah not Amon, like his predecessor. Probably he had transported his capital to Memphis, the sacred city of Ptah or Vulcan, in order to hold the Delta in subjection, in which a revolt of captives had already broken out; and at the same time to defend the frontier against the Canaanites on the East and the Libyans on the West, for the configuration of Egypt is such that the Fayoum once conquered, the narrow slip of land beyond it must inevitably fall into the hands of an invader. Considered as the Pharaoh of the Exodus, it will be at once seen from the political events of the time, how suspicious he was likely to have shown himself towards subjects on his Eastern frontier, whose fidelity he probably suspected, whose numbers and power he feared, and whose affections his father had lost, by the cruel treatment and the slavery to which they had been reduced. The monuments of Menephtah are dated in the first years of his reign, and a tablet of that year at Silsilis, records the offerings made to Amon-Ra, or Amon the Sun, the king of the gods, or Theban Jupiter, and to Hapi, or the Nile, the father of the gods. These gods were associated probably on account of some unusual rise of the river, which had conferred great benefits on the country. Another tablet at Gehl-el-Teir or Sourarieh, inscribed on the walls of the temple of the goddess Athor, has a mention of the Rubu or Libyans, over whom the god Ptah had given the monarch a great victory. The frontiers of Egypt and Libya could not be clearly defined, and were the constant cause of contention. The Libyans had behind them the northern portion of the great continent of Africa, and consisted of several tribes or nations, each governed by its king. Of these nations those known in the inscriptions of this reign were the Rubu or Lubu, the Libyes or Libyans, the Mashauasha, known to the Greeks as the Mazues or Maxues, and the Kahaka, a name extinct at a later period. In the reign of Menephtah, induced probably by the weakness of the Egyptian forces on the West, and the internal distraction of the Delta, these Libyan nations, in alliance with the Sharutana or Sardinians, some of whom had already served as mercenaries in the armies of Rameses II., and the Shakalusha, or

Siculi, the Sicilians, the Tursha, the Tursi or Tyrseni, as the Etruscans were called, the Luka or Lycians, and Akaiusha or Achaioi, the Achæans or Greeks, marched on Egypt. The western part of Egypt had submitted to the barbarians, and it was requisite to defend Heliopolis and Memphis, for the enemy had pushed his advanced guard to the city of Pabaris, north of the port of Horus. Menephtah accordingly assembled his army, which consisted partly of mercenaries, and advanced to give battle. The Libyan king, Marmaiu, son of Deid or Dido, had brought his wife and children with him, and reached a frontier town named Paarisheps. Menephtah harangued his host, and assigned the post of honor to the mercenaries. The god Ptah appeared to him in a dream and foretold him victory. The battle took place on the third of the Egyptian month Epiphi, and for six hours the mercenaries slaughtered the Libyans. Marmaiu fled from the field of battle, on which he had left his bow and quiver, while the oxen, goats, asses, and jewels of his wife, fell into the hands of the Egyptians. The return of the army was triumphant, preceded by asses laden with the hands which had been cut off the slaughtered confederates. Six Libyan generals and 6359 soldiers were killed on the field, besides their Greek allies, the number of which is wanting; but a text at Medinat Habu gives the total of the killed at 12,535 persons. The number of prisoners, comprising the women who had accompanied the Libyan monarch and other princes, amounted to 9376. Besides these an amazing number of weapons, horses, and cattle, were captured, and a portion of the spoil given to the Mashuasha, who were in the Egyptian service, for the Libyans seem to have been divided amongst themselves; and even from the Egyptian account, the brunt of the battle seems to have fallen on the Libyan mercenaries who formed the vanguard of the troops of the Nile. The skin tents and provisions of the enemy were burnt. The battle was probably fought about the eighth year of Menephtah, as the private letters of that date mention the departure of Egyptian officers from Tanis or Pelusium to Paarisheps, apparently to meet the coming war.

In this campaign the name of the Achaians first appears applied to the Greeks, called before Hanebu or Ionians, and does not recur. It has been recognized as the genuine name of the Greeks in the Homeric times, and to have been so for a period not longer than 140 years. The Achaioi do not re-appear in the great confederation of the Khita against Rameses II. in which were included the Mysians, Lycians, and Dardanians, nor do the Sicilians and other Italian people; after that they disappear from history. Hence the wars of Rameses and Menephtah have been considered to be contemporaneous with the war of Troy, and to mark Homer's period in synchronous history. The Khita have been supposed also to be the *Ketaioi* of the Odyssey,* and the Exodus and the Trojan War to have occurred, if

---

* W. E. Gladstone in the Contemporary Review, 1874.

not exactly at the same time, yet closely after one another.

Menephtah continued the construction of Paramessu, and the brick-makers were condemned to send in a certain number every day, the same task to which the Hebrews were compelled under the Pharaoh of the Exodus. As the works of Menephtah, who paid no great attention to Thebes, were chiefly executed in the Delta, they have nearly perished, and this king does not appear important in the annals of the country. It is generally admitted that the Exodus

Portrait of Menephtah, the supposed Pharaoh of the Exodus.
From a statue.

took place in his reign, and that he was the Pharaoh addressed by Moses and Aaron, visited by God with plagues on account of the hardness of his heart, and finally drowned in the Red Sea, in pursuing the Hebrews after their departure from the land of bondage. Lately a new theory has been started about the place from which the Hebrews started. It is supposed to have been from Paramessu or Tanis, and that the Hebrews took the northern route, between the waters of the Lake Serbonis and the Mediterranean, where the sea waters had subsequently engulfed an army of Artaxerxes. Subject of much diversity of opinion, as the tracing of the exact route of the Israelites has ever been, it is difficult to conceive how, from so northern a point the Israelites could have reached the peninsula of Sinai, instead of directing their advance at once upon Canaan and the Jordan.

This theory that the Exodus took place towards the coast of the Mediterranean and not in a direct southern route, towards the Red Sea, has lately been advanced in supposed accordance with the geography of Egypt in the days of Menephtah. It has been asserted that the name of the ancient Zoan was Paramessu or the city of Ramses, the Pharaonic appellative of Zoan, and that Zoan was the later Tanis of the Greek. In accordance with this theory, the Egyptian Pithom is asserted to be the Succoth of the Hebrew narrative. The third station of the Hebrew line of march, Etham, is conjectured to be the Egyptian Khetam or "Fortress," lying to the west of the modern El-Khantereh, or "The Bridge," and on the confines of the desert. From hence they are thought to have directed their course northwards to Migdol, the Magdolon of the Greek and Roman writers, and the modern Tel-es-Semout. Then they encamped between Migdol and the Mediterranean in face of Pihohiroth and before Baal-zephon or the Egyptian Baali Tsapuna, a sanctuary situated close to Mount Kasios. It was along the isthmus, there existing, according to the hypothesis, that the Egyptian army perished in pursuit of the retreating Hebrews as they crossed between the Lake Serbonis or "Serbonian Bog," and the waters of the Mediterranean, amidst "a sea of sea weeds" or reeds, "yam suph," which has often proved fatal to numerous hosts or single travellers. Arrived at Mount Kasios, the Eastern frontier of Egypt, the Hebrews went to Marah or the Bitter Lakes, and from thence to Elim, the Egyptian Aalim or "Fish Town," which lies to the north of the Red Sea. This ingenious hypothesis is supported by circumstantial evidence connected with the history of Joseph and Moses, also by the condition of this part of Egypt in the days of Menephtah, when this Eastern frontier appears to have been denuded of cities, and scarcely occupied by the Egyptians, but left to the Herusha or "Inhabitants of the Desert," as the tribes on this confine were called. The difficulties, however, of reconciling the Scriptural account as to the time passed in the transit as well as that of allowing the philological coincidence of some of the Hebrew and Egyptian names, have caused this brilliant discovery of the supposed direction of the Exodus not to be universally admitted by those who have studied the antiquities of Egypt or Biblical geography.*

* Brugsch-Bey's lecture before the International Congress of

Seti II., also called Menephtah, son of Menephtah and queen Hesineferet, succeeded his father on the throne, but it is not known if his title was not contested, or his rule preceded by another king. Seti II. has not left many memorials of his reign. He erected a small temple at Thebes, and the second year of his reign is mentioned on a pillar at Silsilis, while a tablet at Abusimbel represents him as a conqueror. There is a fine statue of him in the British Museum, found at Thebes; but the name of the god Set has been anciently erased, showing that the introduction of the name of that god, and the substitution in its place of Osiris, was subsequent to his reign. Details are unfortunately wanting in the monuments of the religious struggle between the worshippers of Osiris and Set, which revived the animosities of the Shepherd rule, and ended in chasing Set or Typhon, after it had been adopted by one later king. The reign of Seti II. was perhaps followed by that of Amenmes, of whom little is known, beyond his tomb in the Biban-el-Molook, and the name of his wife. The dynasty was closed by the joint reign of a king named Siphtah and a queen named Tauser or Thousiris, the Thouoris of Manetho. It appears from the inscriptions that Siphtah had been placed on the throne by Bai, and that Siphtah was a native of Kheb, a city of the Aphroditopolite name. Kush was under his power, and Seti, a prince of that country, accompanied by Bai,

Orientalists, 17 September, 1874. Academy, 26 September, 1874, p. 352.

offers his homage to Seti. He was buried in the Biban-el-Molook, or really in the tombs of the kings at Thebes; but his tomb was treated with ignominy and appropriated by his successor.

The interval between the reign of Siphtah and his successor Setnekht was one of great disturbance. It appears from the great Harris papyrus, that a great Exodus took place in Egypt, in consequence of the troubles. "For many years," it states, "there was no master, and for a time the country belonged to the governors of cities, one massacreing another. After a time one Arsu or Areos, a Kharu or Syrian, was chief as it were among them, and the whole country offered him homage, each joining his companion and wasting his goods. And the gods having become as men, no more offerings were made in the temples." How long this state of anarchy continued does not appear, nor by what means the confusion arose, or if it was consequent on the death or usurpation of Siphtah, in whom some recognize Arsu the Syrian. The return of tranquillity was brought about by the gods, who, in order to restore the equilibrium of the country, placed Setnekht on the throne. The actions of Setnekht are summed up in the address of his son Rameses in the same papyrus. "He was like the god Kheper and Set, Typhon, in his rage; he quieted the whole of the country in revolt; he slaughtered the violent who were in Egypt, purified the throne of Egypt, took care to recognize what had been subverted; each saw the brother of those who had been immured; he restored the temples and the divine offerings, so that honors were rendered to the divine orders according to their rights; he promoted me to be heir apparent on the throne of Seb." His name is found at the Sarabit-el-Khadim at Sinai. After this pacification of Egypt and a reign, the length of which is unknown, Setnekht died, and was buried in the tomb of Siphtah in the Biban-el-Molook.

His successor was his son, Rameses III., who followed his father upon the throne. Rameses was one of the most remarkable of the Egyptian kings, and was known to the Greeks by the name of Rampsinitus. From his riches and his power he has been called the Egyptian Solomon. The events of his reign are detailed in the great Harris papyrus, in the address from the throne, which he made to the people of Egypt and the troops. On his elevation to the crown his first task was to reorganize the kingdom. This he did by distributing and reorganizing the castes, officers, chiefs, and army throughout the country. Amongst the soldiers were the Sharutana or Sardinians, and the Kahakas, a tribe or nation of the Libyans. Besides these, his plans embraced the regulation of slaves and other laborers or servants, and the administration or temples. This was necessary after the overthrow of the government which had happened in the Delta. The disposition and organization of the foreigners established in Egypt had become one of the urgent necessities of the political situation. The king proceeds to assert that he had smitten the Danauna coming from their isles, the Tsakkaru and the Pulesta. "The Sharutana or Sardinians, and Cashasha of the sea, were reduced to non-existence." They were taken at a blow, and led captive "in numbers like the sands of the torrents," to Egypt. They were placed under guard with their numerous families in a fortified city. These events happened in the eighth year of his reign, and were probably, on account of their importance, placed before some which will be mentioned, and happened after; for the first task of Rameses was to repulse the Shasu or Shepherds, whose sinister reappearance threatened again the existence of Egypt. The Mashausha, who had permanently established themselves in the Delta, revolted, attacked the principal towns, desolated the country, and advanced beyond Memphis to a city named Karbana; they went as far as the "great river," and established themselves for years as masters of the Fayoum. Rameses attacked and drove them back, after a fearful battle, in which there were heaps of the slain Mashausha, who were confederated with the Libyans in the fifth year of his reign. In this campaign, signalized alike by the hosts of the dead and the number of prisoners, the king was accompanied by the "Council of the Thirty," while the enemy had been excited to revolt by five chiefs, named Taiti or Didi, Mashaken, Maraiu, Gamar and Gautmar, whose names are mentioned in the inscription of Medinat Habu. In this war followed the usual mutilation of the dead, analogous to that described in Scripture, as inflicted on the living by the

K

king of Bezek. "Adoni-bezek fled: and they pursued after him, and cut off his thumbs and his great toes. And Adoni-bezek said, Threescore and ten kings, having their thumbs and great toes cut off, gathered their meat under my table."* This attack on the Mashuasha only repulsed them for a while, and it appears that Rameses had about the same time to repulse the Satu or Asiatics. In his eighth year he had to resist the maritime nations, who again attacked Egypt. "They had cast their eyes" on Egypt. The enemy had this time come from the isles of the Mediterranean. They had subdued the Khita or supposed Hittites, the Kati, the Karkamasha or people of Carchemish, Aradu or Aradus, and Aras, and pitched their camp in the midst of the land of Amaur, or the Amorites, south-west of the Dead Sea. These maritime people, like the invaders in the days of Menephtah, consisted of the confederated Pulusata or Pelasgi, the Tsekkariu or Teucrians, the Shakalusha or Sicilians, the Tanau or Daunians, and the Uashasha or Osci. They had threatened the Asiatic frontiers of Egypt. Rameses concentrated an army at Taha in Palestine, consisting of Egyptian and mercenary or tributary soldiery, and assembled a considerable fleet at the mouth of the Nile. In the pictures representing this campaign, the Egyptian vessels are depicted sinking the ships of the enemy; while four of the sons of Rameses, and the monarch himself, armed, shoot down with their bows the enemy from the shore, for the enemy had entered the

* Judges i. 6, 7.

mouth of the Nile. This great war is represented in seven pictures, sculptured on the walls of Medinet Habu. In these, Rameses is depicted haranguing the Egyptian officers, announcing to them the war, and distributing arms to the troops which he has raised to repulse the enemy. The march of the Egyptian army is then seen, the monarch in his war chariot preparing for the struggle. The first victory of the Egyptians, was the slaying of the Pelasgi or Teukri, some of whom are in cars drawn by four oxen. These Teukri and Pelasgi have a peculiar head-dress, surmounted by plumes, like that of the Egyptian god Besa, and also found on the head of certain figures on the stair-case of Persepolis. This scene is followed by another, in which Rameses enters a place filled with lions,* which probably impeded his army, as that of Xerxes is said to have been at Mount Athos by the same beasts. Rameses destroys them from his chariot like the Assyrian kings in the reliefs of Kouyunjik. This place is supposed to correspond to Southern Palestine, which abounded in lions in the days of Samson, David, and Jeroboam†. The naval battle is the subject of the fifth picture, and has been already described. It appears to have taken place after the defeat of the enemy by land. In the description of the action at sea, it is stated in the text that the natives who had come from the isles of the Great Sea

* 1 Sam. vi. 7-12.
† Judges xiv. 5; 1 Samuel xvii. 34; 2 Samuel xxiii. 20; 1 Kings xiii. 24.

or Mediterranean, were taken as in a net, and fallen in the mouth of the Nile. For the sake of defending Egypt from the attack, the king had returned from his frontiers in the land of Taha after the battle with the Pulusta and their confederates, to defend the mouths of the Nile. This land of Taha was a part of Palestine in which was comprised Amaur or the Amorites. After the victory Rameses counted the hands cut off the dead bodies of the fallen enemy at the Makataru or Migdol of Rameses, the fortified city of the same name as that mentioned as built by the Hebrews. It is clear that the fortress could not have been distant from the Egyptian frontier, as the slaves who fled from Egypt had to pass its ramparts. After his victory Rameses led his European captives to the temple of Amon at Thebes. In this expedition the Pelasgi had been united with the Tursha or Etruscans, the Pelasgi at that time having issued from Samothrace, and colonized the isles of the Archipelago and Ægean as well as Crete and the shores of Caria, the Teucrians occupying the northern coasts of Asia Minor, and the Tursha or Turseni, the western coasts of Italy, where they had early introduced writing into Latium. It is remarkable, however, to find them so named at so early a period, as the Etruscans called themselves Rasenna.

The European nations of this period were only partially provided with defensive armor, such as the helmet and the shield. The Sardinians may have worn the breast-plate, but no greaves, as mentioned in Homer, are seen; while the plume is absent from the helmet, or replaced by horns such as the Gauls and Thracians are said to have worn, or else by a globe and horns, perhaps an emblem of Astarte. The Etruscans had the pointed helmet, seen in the monuments of that people. All used circular or Argolic bucklers, and for offensive weapons, swords or lances. The head attire of the other Italic and Greek races is unlike that ever seen on the monuments of these people. The ships of the Egyptians and their enemies, as represented in the pictures, have one mast, and a square sail lowered by cords on the deck by halyards, the mast and crow's nest in which the look-out was kept; the galleys only a single bank of oars, the prows end in the heads of animals as in the Greek galleys.

After the war with the European nations, another broke out with the Libyans in his eleventh year. The expressions of the victory of the king are poetic. "The enemy," it is said, "were hid like birds before a hawk who darts from his hiding-place in the midst of the wood." It continues, "they came as to a slaughter-house, and fell under the grip of the king like rats." The leaders of this war were the Mashuasha, Maxyes or Mazyes, who had again invaded Egypt urged on by the Tahennu or Numidians. They were led by their monarch Kapur, and after a battle appear to have surrendered; but Kapur was killed in the struggle, apparently when taken prisoner, and his son Mashashar surrendered unconditionally to Rameses. The Libyans lost 4227 killed or taken prisoners, of which last 538 were women, which naturally suggests that these were, in fact, migratory movements of Libyan people defeated by their neighbors, and forced to seek a refuge or new home in the valley of the Nile. Numerous weapons and a small number of horses and cattle fell as spoil to the Egyptians. The Mashuasha, who appear to have inhabited the Cyrenaica or Marmarica, the Marmaris of Strabo, were incorporated with Egypt, and supplied mercenary troops for the service of the Pharaohs. They are mentioned in the Scriptures as the support of No-ammon, and the allies of Egypt and Ethiopia.* Their princes were hereditary, and carried on war in person. Their names will continue to appear in history. These victories had so assured the tranquillity of Egypt that the scribe exclaims at the end of one inscription: "The earth is like a birth without pains; let the woman go forth when she likes, let her adorn herself according to her inclinations, and boldly walk where she choose," which has been compared with the words of Isaiah, "Pass through thy land as a river, oh daughter of Tarshish, there is no more strength."† In the Harris papyrus the tribes of the Libyans mentioned are the Rubu or Libu, the Libyans, the Sabata, the Kaikasha, the Shai, the Hasu, and the Bakana. These have been supposed to represent the different tribes of Numidia and Mauritania, but their names cannot be identi-

---

* See Nahum iii. 9; Daniel xi. 43; 2 Kings xvi. 8; Ezek. xxvii. 10; xxx. 5.

† Isaiah xxiii. 10.

fied with those otherwise recorded. Besides recruiting the armies they also manned the fleets of Egypt. In the Eastern states Rameses had made a great reservoir in the country of Ainau, surrounded by a wall sunk in the earth to the depth of thirty cubits, with quays and doors of cedar-wood with bronze bolts, supposed to be Beersheba, halfway from Hebron to Rehoboth, on the road to Syria. He had also despatched a fleet to Arabia, which had returned laden with the spices and gums of Arabia to Coptos, and thence carried them on the backs of men and asses to Thebes. To the foundries of Ataka* he had sent also ships, which returned laden with bricks or ingots of brass of the color of gold. To the goddess Athor he had dedicated her temple of the Sarabit-el-Khadim bringing thence quantities of *mafka*, supposed to be the turquoise. This temple still continued to be the principal station of this Egyptian colony. The expedition of Rameses is recorded on the spot by the sculptures still remaining on the walls of the temple of the goddess. Egypt, it appears, had been reduced to safety and tranquillity, the country and army had been reorganized. But the people are described as receiving their daily sustenance from the Pharaoh, in return for their labor, as if the land entirely belonged to the monarch.† Rameses had also carried on war against the Ethiopians, and conquered the Taraui and the Amari. The works of Ra-

* Perhaps the Athak of 1 Samuel xxx. 30; xlii. 20, 21.
† See Gen. xlvii.

meses are of great beauty and extent, and the Harris papyrus records the enormous gifts he made during his reign to the temples of Ptah at Memphis, of Tum at Heliopolis, and of Amon at Medinat Habu. It is at this part of Thebes his conquests are sculptured, and a calendar marked the fixed year or the rising of the Dog-star on the first day of the month Thoth, the new-year's day of Egypt, about 1300 B. C. Nine of his sons are here recorded, some of whom succeeded to the crown; and his treasury, on the walls of which are depicted and recorded his riches, is that described by Herodotus in his sensational account of the life of Rampsindus. Besides his riches and his martial exploits, Rameses appears to have been addicted to sensual indulgence, which gave rise to the caricatures and sarcasms of his contemporaries. His visit to Hades and his playing at draughts with Isis, was apparently a myth, derived from an imperfect understanding of the sculptures. After a reign just exceeding thirty-one years, Rameses was buried in a stone sarcophagus placed in a large and magnificent tomb in the Biban-el-Molook. But the "irony of fate," as it has been sometimes styled, has transported the lid of his granite coffin to the Fitz-William Museum, of Cambridge, and the endowment papyrus roll of his temples to a table case in the British Museum. He was the last of the great heroic kings of Egypt, uniting in his person the valor of David with the luxury of Solomon. The domestic repose of Rameses was disturbed by a conspiracy in the palace in which the intrigues of Penhuiban, an officer of the court played an important part. He made use of magical figures of wax, written charms or incantations, talismans, and other enchantments, and fascinated the females of the palace to enter into a conspiracy against the life of the monarch. The conspiracy against the Pharaoh comprised ten officers, and six women of the palace who had combined with them for the purpose. Besides the principal conspirators, several others had participated in a greater or less degree, and had listened to, without denouncing to the authorities, the proposals of the principal conspirators. Amongst them appear Ethiopians and foreign officers of the mercenary troops, who had entered the service of Egypt. One of the royal family was implicated in the treasonable plot. They were detected and examined before the king in council, a kind of criminal tribunal or commission, constituted of twelve judges or persons of high rank, such as the treasurers, the standard-bearers, and the royal scribes or secretaries of state, nominated by the monarch for the special purpose. The accused were subjected to interrogation, and the punishment of death was inflicted on the most culpable, amongst whom were Penhuiban, his accomplice Penbakakamen, and one Pentaur, a scion of royalty. In some instances the extreme penalty of death was commuted for one hardly less merciful, the cutting off the nose and ears of offenders, one that at some time or other has prevailed in all countries. The judicial papyrus of Turin, which records this episode of the life of Rameses, has its date unfortunately torn off, so that it is uncertain when it happened, probably indeed towards the close of the reign of this illustrious monarch.

His son Rameses IV. mounted the throne after him, apparently at a youthful age. Little is known of the events of his reign. He founded a station at El Hammamat in his second year, and the highest date found of his reign is his eighteenth year. Consequent probably upon some revolution, Rameses V. succeeded as a usurper to the throne. He has left a tablet of some benefits conferred on Silsilis. His successor, Rameses VI., was not more distinguished than his predecessor, and the most interesting monument of his reign is his tomb, constructed in the Biban-el-Molook. On the ceiling is a list of star-risings, amongst others that of the Sothis or Dog-star, calculated at 1240 B. C. The only other monument of his reign is a tomb at a place anciently called Shaa, now Anibe, near Para, or the modern Deru. In it Punnu, a prince of Kush or Ethiopia, offers to Rameses VI. a royal statue of the monarch. Punnu, it appears, was a native of Uaut, apparently known to the Greeks as *Aue*. The king, it appears, had conquered or held subject the countries of Ahi and Akaka, reduced to subjection by the prince of Ethiopia. His successors, Rameses VII. and Rameses VIII., were insignificant monarchs. A royal scribe, named Horus, formerly a slave in the town of Mendes, has just recorded his reign in a sepulchral tablet, dedicated to the deities Onouris, Osiris, and Horus. According to some he was followed on the throne by Meritum, the seventh son of Rameses III., and succeeded by the equally unimportant Rameses IX. The reign of Rameses IX. was disturbed by the sacrilege of the tombs of the ancient kings, which had been broken into and plundered by robbers in the sixteenth year of his reign, and it appears that these had been preceded by other violations, and continued till his nineteenth year, and a commission was appointed to examine the condition of the tombs and try the offenders. Ten sepulchres of kings, including one of the queen Isis at Drah-abu-el-Neggah, were examined. They comprised those of some of the Antefs, or monarchs of the eleventh dynasty; that of Sebakemsaf of the succeeding line, Taakan of the seventeenth, and Amenophis I. of the eighteenth dynasty. Six members composed the commission, and amongst them were the governor of the district, a magistrate, and a royal officer. Some of the tombs were broken into, but that of Sebakemsaf was particularly injured, the coffin violated, and the royal mummy thrown on the ground. It appears that eight robbers were engaged in the spoliation, and that after having stripped the mummies of their gold ornaments, they burnt the royal coffins. The accused were subjected to the interrogatory in prison, and the commission of six subsequently augmented to twelve members, the usual number of judges, the high-priest of Amon and other functionaries having been placed upon it. The accused were acquitted, but it appears from another document that the eight engaged in the spoliation, perhaps afterwards discovered, were bastinadoed or put to death. After his nineteenth year this Rameses, the successor of Rameses VII., associated his son in the government of the country.

Rameses IX. was succeeded by the Rameses X. and XI., monarchs whose names are just found on the monuments, but who performed no action or left behind them no works worthy of record. It has been supposed that, like the mayors of the palace in France, the high-priests of Amon at Thebes usurped the authority of these short-lived kings; but this was probably owing to domestic discords, and the revolution of the palace, which undermined the family and abridged their reigns.

Rameses XII., who came to the throne after the last king, is known by a remarkable inscription. A tablet, found in the temple to the east of the palace of the south-western quarter of Karnak, dedicated to the god Khons, a personification of the moon, and the son of Amon and Nut, contains an account of the principal event of this reign. The temple had been erected by the previous monarch, and in it were the living cynocephali, apes, the sacred animals of the Khons, under the charge of a priest of the god. The picture of the tablet represents Rameses holding a censer, worshipping the ark of the god, which partially covered with curtains, is placed on a boat terminating at each end in the bust of Khons. Figures of priests, a sphinx, and standards are in the boat, behind it is a standard and flabellum, while twelve priests carry it upon their shoulders.* In this ark the figure of the god was enshrined, and the scene, as will be subsequently shown, depicts his departure from Egypt.

Another scene represents the return of Khons, the ark borne by four and met by another priest. It appears from the inscription that the king had been in the land of Nehar, collecting or receiving the annual revenues or tributes, and that the lands had obediently rendered them; each of the chiefs or princes vieing with one another in submission, and bringing the usual tribute imposed by the Egyptians, gold and silver, lapis lazuli or glass khesbet, the blue or green ores, or turquoise requisite for the blue colors, and porcelain of Egypt, and all the good or fragrant wood of Taneter or the "Holy Land," as Arabia was then called, "upon their backs." This term, "Holy Land," was applied by the later prophets to Palestine, then designated in the Hebrew *admata hakhodesh*.† The chief of Bakhtan was amongst the tributaries, and he offered in addition to his other tributes his daughter, who "being a very beautiful person, his majesty prized her above all things." Rameses, who was probably at that time a mere youth, took her for his wife, and changed her name to Ra-neferu, or "Most beautiful Sun." On his return to Egypt the marriage rites were duly solemnized, although it is unfortunate the ceremonies necessary for an Egyptian marriage are unknown. On the 22d of the month

---

* Like the arks of the Moabites, Amos v. 26.
† Zechariah ii. 12.

Epiphi, of the fifteenth year of his reign, when Rameses was in the Thebaid, an envoy of Bakhtan came with presents to the king. "I have come to thee, my lord," he said, "on account of Bentaresh, the younger sister of thy royal wife Ra-neferu, who is unable to move, would your majesty let a royal scribe see her." The king ordered the college of sacred scribes, the *rekhkhet*, and the doctors of mysteries or magic, the *rekh-get-amon*,* "those acquainted with hidden words," to be sent for, and when they had come—"Show me," he said, "a man of intelligent heart and skilful with his fingers, one of your number." They pointed out the royal scribe, Tetemhebi, and the king sent him with the envoy to the land of Bakhtan. Tetemhebi found the princess was possessed with an evil spirit or demon, but he was unable to cope with it. Upon this the king of Bakhtan sent again, in his twenty-sixth year, to ask for aid. Rameses consulted in this strait Khons of Thebes, to order Khons, the giver of counsels or oracles, to go to Bakhtan to cure the princess. The god nodded or assented, and despatched the second Khons, as he must be called, who departed in an ark, accompanied by five other arks and a chariot, and escorted by a troop of cavalry. The journey occupied seventeen months, and on the arrival in the country, the king of Bakhtan accompanied by his guards, prostrated himself, and saluted the god. When Khons was brought to the place where Benta-

* These are the chartummin of Exodus.

resh was, his presence expelled the spirit and cured the princess. The exorcised demon exclaimed, "Great god, who chasest demons, thou hast come in peace. The fortress of Bakhtan is thine, its inhabi-

Departure of the Ark of the God Khons to the land of Bakhtan.

tants are thy slaves. I return whence I came to satisfy thee for thy journey. Would your sanctity order that a festival should be made in my honor by the king of the Bakhtan." The god accorded the request by the mouth of the prophet who accompanied him, and the king, alarmed at the interview between the god and the spirit, prepared the feast, only too happy to see the departure of the evil spirit. This work of thaumaturgy having been performed, the king of Bakhtan was unwilling that the god Khons should return to Egypt, and wished to retain him at his capital, when the god gave another manifestation of his power. After a detention of three years and nine months, Khons appeared in a vision to the king while reclining on his couch, and assumed the appearance of a golden hawk coming out of his ark and flying towards Egypt. Agitated and convulsed, on his awakening he sent for the priest of the god. "Let him quit us," he said, "and depart towards Egypt, make ready the chariot for Egypt." Not unmindful of the benefits conferred, or awed by the power of the god, the king gave rich and numerous presents to the god, and soldiers and horses, probably to escort him in safety to the Thebaid. When Khons the counsellor arrived at the temple of Khons, he offered to him all the presents which he had received, and re-entered his own chapel or temple in peace, on the nineteenth Mechir, in the thirty-third year of the monarch's reign. Bakhtan is supposed to be either Bagestan or Ecbatana, and the inscription shows the intimate relations which existed between the Egyptian and Asiatic monarchs, and the mutual influence of the idolatries of Egypt and Asia upon each other. Rameses XIII. closes the list of the twentieth dynasty, at this time effete or extinct.* The high-

* There is an official letter of the seventeenth year of his reign addressed to his son Painehsi.

priests of Amon took command of the troops as well as of the temples, and assumed the serpent diadem, the badge of royalty. One of these high-priests, who lived in the reign of this last Rameses, at last mounted the throne and founded a new dynasty.

L

CHAPTER IV.

FROM THE TWENTY-FIRST DYNASTY TO THE CONQUEST.

From about 1100 B. C. to 332 B. C.

THE Theban line of the Ramessids appears to have been broken up by the complete usurpation of the throne by the high-priests of Amon. It has been supposed that three contemporary dynasties were existing in Egypt at the time, as it is difficult to reconcile the lists of Manetho of the kings of the twenty-first dynasty with the monuments. In the first place it will be desirable to follow the Theban line of king-priests who assumed the sovereign power. The first of these was Harhor, high-priest of Amon in the reign of Rameses XII. The only historical points of his reign are the submission of the Rutennu or Northern Syrians, and his marriage with a Semitic female, by whom he had several sons bearing Semitic names. He does not appear to have established the government in his own family, and was succeeded by his grandson Painetem, who was married to a princess named Rakemaa, of the Ramessid line, and thus acquired a kind of legitimate title to the throne. But some difficulty pervades the exact knowledge of this part of the history of Egypt, and the same or another Painetem, with a prenomen and another wife, intrudes on the monuments of Egypt. The last sacerdotal monarch of this line is Ramenkheper. His name and that of his wife Hesiemkheb have been found on the bricks of Kheb in the Heptanomide. The names supposed to correspond to those in the lists of Manetho are those of the king Pasiuenkha or *Psinaches*, and another Harpasebensha. During the twentieth dynasty the Hebrews are supposed, guided by the judges, to have established themselves in Palestine, and founded their monarchy, and Solomon to have sent for an Egyptian wife to one of these Tanite princes. That king had taken the town of Guzer and burnt it, slaughtering the Canaanite garrison. It was from Egypt at this period that Solomon and the contemporary kings of the Khita and Syrians imported chariots and horses, at the rate of 600 pieces of silver for a chariot and 150 for the horses. No information as to the period of the twenty-first dynasty is afforded by the Apis tablets. If the history of the twenty-first dynasty is obscure, that of the twenty-second, or Bubastite dynasty as it has been called, is not less difficult. According to Manetho it consisted of nine kings, who reigned 116 years. The first of these monarchs was the Sheshanka of the Egyptians, Shishak of the Hebrews, and Sesonchosis of the Greeks. His family was of Libyan or Semitic origin, and descended from Psusennes. The names of his descendants, as will be subsequently seen, identify them with the great Chaldean families which reigned over Assyria and Babylonia. It is in this reign that the web of Egyptian and Hebrew history again becomes interwoven. Jeroboam, one of the officers of Solomon, revolted against him. Designated by the prophet Ahijah* as the future king of Israel, Solomon sought to kill him, Jeroboam fled to the court of Shishak for protection, as Hadad the son of the king of Edom had previously done, and married into the royal family of Egypt, both Hadad and Jeroboam being the avowed enemies of Solomon. After the death of Solomon Jeroboam, supported by the Egyptian interest, returned and was elected king of Israel, while Rehoboam obtained only the kingdom of Judah. Alarmed at the state of affairs he fortified the principal cities, but in the fifth year of his reign Shishak marched with an army of 1200 chariots, 60,000 horsemen, and a numerous infantry, composed of the Mashuash or Libyans, Nubians, Ethiopians, and Egyptians, to the attack of Jerusalem.† The host of Shishak is supposed to have penetrated Judah in three columns, and Shishak took and pillaged Jerusalem, taking the treasures of the temple and the palace, and golden bucklers which Solomon had made probably for his body-guard. On the walls of the so-called portico of the Bubastites at Karnak Shishak has recorded more than 130 cities which he had taken, given to him by Amon and the goddess of the Thebaid.

* 1 Kings xi. 14-40. † 1 Kings xiii. 25-26.

Amongst the cities which can be recognised in the hieroglyphic legends are Rabboth, Taanach, Sunem, Rehob, Hapharaim, Adoraim, Mahanaim, Gibeon, Beth-Horon, Kedemoth, Ajalon, Megiddo, and Judah Maluk, "the royal city of Judah," or Jerusalem.

Although, owing to the dilapidations of the wall, the whole of the names cannot be read, it is evident that the arms of Shishak were carried into Palestine. Unfortunately the year of his reign in which he invaded that country is not known, so as to give the synchronism of the history of the two countries. Shishak did not, however, reign more than twenty-one years, so that it must have happened before that date. His successor Uasarkan or Osorchon I. may have been named after the Assyrian name Sargon; his reign was insignificant, an observation which equally applies to that of Takarut or Takalut, Takellothis I. It is about the period of these reigns that the invasion of Judah by the Ethiopian monarch Serach and his Kushite and Libyan hosts, defeated by the king of Judah at Tsezphath, near Maresa, is placed by some. Uasarkan or Osorchon II. was equally undistinguished during his long reign. The mention of an eclipse of the moon, which was expected or happened, occurs in an inscription of his successor This took place on the twenty-fourth of the month Choiak of his fifteenth year. The mutilated inscription which records it also mentions disturbances which happened at the time; records the victories of the king in the South and North; refers to some more operations, and the festivals and offerings made in honor of the gods of Thebes and Hermonthis. In the twenty-third year of his reign one of the bulls of Apis died, and was buried with great pomp in the Serapeum by his son Shishak, at that time governor of Memphis. Search was made for another of these sacred bulls after the seventy days of embalming and mourning had expired. Osorchon left two sons behind him. The youngest, named Namrut or Nimrod, after his Assyrian ancestors, was high-priest of Amon, and commanded the army stationed at Heracleopolis. His eldest son, Shishak II., his successor, is scarcely known from the monuments. His nephew, Takarut or Takelut, Takelothis II., son of Nimrod, succeeded, and appears to have been associated in the government with his predecessors. Some long but mutilated inscriptions, dated in the eleventh year of his reign, towards the close of which his wife Karumamma, a statue of whom is in the Louvre, died, are known. The texts mention the rise of Sothis or the Dog-star, and the offerings of gold and other objects made to the temple of Amon and the gods of Thebes. Another inscription of the same date is known about a deceased prince Uasarkan. An Apis died in his fifteenth year.

Sheshanka III. reigned fifty-one years, and all that is known of his rule is that an Apis was born in the twenty-eighth year, showing that another had died about the period. An inscription of the portico of the Bubastites of the same date mentions the rich gifts he made to the temple of Amon at Thebes. His successor Pamai is only known by the tablet of the bull Apis at the Serapeum, the Apis born in the twenty-eighth year of his predecessor having died in the twentieth year of his reign at the age of twenty-six years. Pamai was succeeded by Sheshanka IV. who reigned thirty-six years more, during which three of the sacred bulls died, in the fourth, eleventh, and twenty-seventh year of his reign. With this monarch the twenty-second dynasty closed.

It would appear that after Sheshanka IV., Egypt had fallen into the power of the Ethiopians, having previously, from some unexplained causes, broken up into a number of small states. These were under the protection or government of Piankhi, an Ethiopian monarch residing at Noph or Napata. In the twenty-first year of his reign, in the month of Thoth, a messenger came to inform the king that Tafnekht, commander of the foreign troops, chief or monarch of the nome Menouthes, had revolted and made himself master of Lower Egypt, and extended his sway as far as Heracleopolis. One of the principal chiefs who had been conquered was prince Nimrod of Hermopolis. On the receipt of this intelligence, Piankhi sent reinforcements to the chiefs who remained faithful to him, and embarking his troops on the Nile, sailed down towards Thebes, and met on their way the army of the North, which Piankhi's forces rapidly defeated. The Northern troops fled to Sutensenen or Heracleopolis. The confederated rebels consisted of the princes Nimrod and Uaput, the prince Osorchon of Bubastis,

Sheshanka, the prince Bakennifi, and some chiefs of the Libyans, and other mercenaries under Tafnekht. The prince Nimrod was ascending the river southwards when he heard of the advance of the Ethiopians, and at once fled into the port of Hermopolis. After some partial but imperfect successes of his troops, Piankhi left his Ethiopian capital and arrived at Thebes. He harangued and rebuked his army from his war chariot. He then proceeded to besiege Hermopolis, raising works against it, and after three days Hermopolis, overcome by the stench of the dead, surrendered.

Surrender of Nimrod and other Princes to Piankhi.

Envoys were sent by Nimrod to treat with Piankhi. After them Nimrod "sent his wife, a queen by marriage and birth, named Nestennest, to offer homage to the king's wives, concubines, daughters and sisters, and to prostrate herself in the female apartments before the king's wives. 'I am come,' she said, 'oh, queens and princesses, do you reconcile the divine king, lord of the palace, whose spirit is mighty, and whose justice is great.'"

Nimrod himself subsequently came, leading his horse by a bridle in his right hand and holding a sistrum in his left. Piankhi entered Hermopolis and examined the treasury, store-houses, and stables. Piankhi was exceedingly vexed at the state of the horses, and their starved condition, which could scarcely have been due to the siege. Pefaabast, the chief, prince of Heracleopolis, subsequently surrendered, and offered his riches and the choicest of his stud to Piankhi. The haughty Ethiopian averted his face from the wives of the Egyptian. The cities of Pa-ra-sekhem-kheper and Mertum surrendered without a blow. His victorious march was directed to Memphis, but Tafnekht hastened to reinforce it with 8000 men, and strengthened its eastern fortifications. Tafnekht after two days' stay retreated to the north, and Piankhi advanced to the siege of Memphis, and came in his ship to the north of the city, and as there was a high Nile, brought his fleet close under the walls of the city.

The city was taken by assault, and after a great slaughter, he re-entered the city and sacrificed to the god Ptah. Uaput, Merkaneshu, and Petesis, with a considerable portion of the northern confederation, surrendered. From Memphis Piankhi proceeded to

Heliopolis, where he bathed in the lake, and offered a sacrifice to Ra at sunrise on the dunes. He then went to the temple of the god Ra, and was purified by the high-priest; after this ceremony he ascended the steps to the great shrine in the temple, and alone drew the bolts and opened the folding doors, and beheld the boats of Ra and Tum. He then sealed the doors with a clay seal* and said, "I have set my seal, let no other king whatever enter therein." The prince Uasarkan then came to the king, who proceeded to Kaken, and Petesis surrendered, invited Piankhi to his palace, and gave up all his treasures, declaring with an oath that none had been reserved or concealed. The whole of the land had gradually fallen into the power of Piankhi; but Tafnekht fled to the islands of the Mediterranean, probably Cyprus, whence he sent envoys to the conqueror, and two Ethiopian envoys went to Tafnekht, who took the oath of allegiance. This completed the general submission of the northern chiefs, and the suppression of the revolt. Four sovereigns, two of the North and two of the South, rendered homage to Piankhi, but were not allowed to enter the palace because they were eaters of fish. Nimrod, however, who was not addicted to that unclean food, was admitted. With a rich booty, amongst which are reckoned the products of Kharu or Syria, and Taneter or Arabia, Piankhi ascended the Nile in triumph to Thebes.

As the narrative stands, Piankhi appears to have

---

* Cf. Daniel vi. 17, also the apocryphal Bel and the Dragon 14.

been distinguished for his devotion to the god Amon, and the moderation he displayed towards the conquered. Apart from the necessities of war he seems to have shown no vindictive feeling either to the revolted princes or the assaulted cities. Although it is usual to consider that the invasions of Piankhi preceded the reign of Bokchoris, some doubts are thrown on the actual period of the invasion, by the fact that the names of many of the monarchs and governors of cities reappear in the Assyrian annals of Assurbanipal at a later date; and that it is within the verge of probability that Piankhi might have preceded Sabaco and not Bokchoris, as is usually assumed by those who have hitherto treated the subject of this reign. The twenty-second dynasty was succeeded by the twenty-third or Tanite, and consisted, according to Manetho, of four kings, who reigned eighty-nine years. Petsabast or Petoubustes was the first monarch. According to Manetho he reigned forty years, but no important monument of his time remains. Uasarkan or Osorchon, the second monarch, reigned eight years, and Psænmut or Psammus ten. The last king of Manetho, Zet, has not been discovered, although a reign of thirty-one years has been assigned to him. The tablets of the Serapeum throw no light on this dark spot of Egyptian history, for no Apis is recorded either to have been born or died in their reigns. From this it would appear that they were local contemporaries of the Ethiopians and the twenty-fourth dynasty, which consisted of a single king named Bakenranef or Bokchoris, native of

Sais, and son of Tafnekht or Tnephachthes. He is stated to have been feeble in body, but wise, intelligent, and avaricious of gain. As a statesman he passed laws about the interests of money, and the succession to the crown; and his sayings attained great popularity. A monstrous ram, with eight feet, two heads, four horns, and two tails, is said to have spoken in his reign, supposed to refer to some mythological event, as also the combat of the bull Mnevis and another bull provoked by the king. He reigned six years, and the Apis which died in that year is mentioned in the hieroglyphic legends, and one buried in the same chamber with the bull which died in the thirty-seventh year of Sheshank IV., showing that Bokchoris succeeded that king at Memphis. Notwithstanding his wisdom he was unable to resist the arms of the Ethiopians, who advancing under their king Sabaco, took Bokchoris captive, and burnt him alive, about B.C. 715. From this period the contemporaneous history of Assyria is known from the Cuneiform inscriptions, which throw great and unexpected light upon the relations of Egypt, both to the kingdoms of Israel, Judah, and the kingdom of Assyria. At this time the preponderance of Assyria appears fixed in the neighborhood of Egypt, which it prepared to attack. Shalmaneser approached the frontiers of Egypt, attacked the kingdom of Israel, and took Samaria in the ninth year of Hoshea. The general of the Assyrian king reproached Hoshea for resting on the staff of this bruised reed, even Egypt, on which if a man

NEW EMPIRE.

lean, it will go into his hand and pierce it, so is Pharaoh king of Egypt and all who trust on him."* It was in vain that Hoshea applied to So,† the Ethiopian monarch who then ruled Egypt, and who afforded him no assistance.

The weakness of Egypt led to the conquest of Samaria by the Assyrians, and the carrying away of the ten lost tribes. Shabaka or Sabaco, the first of the recognized monarchs of the twenty-fifth or Ethiopian dynasty of Manetho, was a native of Akesh, in Kush or Ethiopia. His name is found on the temple at Karnak. He was the contemporary of Sargon, and the king who burnt alive the unfortunate Bokchoris. He is mentioned by Herodotus, and retired from Egypt in consequence of a dream. The death of an Apis is recorded in the second year of his reign at the Serapeum, and his name is found on the monuments of Karnak. He concluded a treaty with one of the Assyrian monarchs, and the seal which was attached to it was found in the archives of Kouyunjik, the ancient Nineveh. His reign is supposed to have lasted eight years. The successor of Shabaka, named

Clay seal of Shabaka or Sabaco. Found at Nineveh.

Shabatuk, the Sebichos of the Greek list and Sibahi

* 2 Kings xviii. 21. † Ibid. 4.

of the Assyrian annals, must have reigned about ten years. Sibahi, according to the Assyrian annals, marched to the assistance of Khanunu king of Gaza; but the confederates were defeated at the battle of Raphia, from which Sibahi escaped. Probably the power of Sibahi was not recognized by the Assyrians, for they do not call him king in their annals. Taharka or Tirharka, whose sister Sabaco had married, ascended the throne. He was soon at war with the Assyrians. About ten years after the capture of Samaria, Hezekiah threw off his allegiance from Sennacherib, and asked the assistance of Tirhakah to expel the Assyrians, and Sennacherib marched on Judæa. Sennacherib, it appears, subsequently retired after having reduced Hezekiah once more to submission. In the subsequent reign of Esarhaddon, B. C. 672, Tirhakah stirred up Bahal king of Tyre to revolt against the supremacy of Assyria. To defeat this combination Esarhaddon marched to Palestine and laid siege to Tyre, in a tenth campaign which he had made during his reign.* He himself marched from Aphek in Lebanon, along the coast of Palestine to Raphia, for a distance of about 200 miles; and the king of Arabia supplied his forces with water. They suffered intensely from the effects of thirst, till they reached the banks of the father of waters, the Nile. Once arrived in Egypt, in the twenty-third year of Tirhakah, he rapidly became master of the country, and took Thebes, annexing the whole of the country to Assyria. The object of Esarhaddon was the con-

* Athenæum, June 20, 1874, p. 829.

quest of Meroe, which it is uncertain if he ever reached. On the rocks of the Nahr-el-Kelb, "Dog river," near Beirout, he carved a tablet close to those of Rameses II., recording his march through that defile to Egypt, traversing the route of the former conquerors of Assyria. Tirhakah continued the struggle for the possession of Egypt with Esarhaddon.

It must have been about this time that Esarhaddon organized Egypt as a subject kingdom, under local princes or governors, dividing the country into twenty nomes or districts. The names of some of the rulers were Assyrian, and those of the cities were changed into others of the same language. The names recorded in the Assyrian annals are Niku or Necho, king of Memphis and Sais, the principal monarch, Sarru-etiq-dairi, king of Zianu or Tanis, Pasankhuru, king of Natku, Pakruru, king of Pisabtu, Pukhuniniapi, king of Khatkiribi or Athribis, Nakh-ke, king of Khininsi or Heracleopolis, Patubisti or Petubastes, king of Zanu, Unamunu or Unamen, king of Nalakhu, Kharsiyesu or Harsiesis, king of Zabnuti, Puaima or Puma, king of Bendidi or Mendes, Sasingu, Sheshank or Shishak, king of Busiru, Tapnakhti or Tnephakhthes, king of Bunu, Pakhunaniapi, Iphkhardesu, or Heptharesis, king of Pizattikhurunpi, Nakhti-kharu-anshini or Nekhtharenshen, king of Pisabtinuti, Pakurninip king of Pakhnuti, Tsikha king of Siayut or Lycopolis, Lamentu, king of Khimuni, Chemmis, or Panopolis, Ispimagu, king of Taini or Thynis, Mantumi-ankhu or Mentuemankh, king of Nia or Thebes. It is remarkable that a similar kind of government prevailed under the Mamelukes in 1783: Egypt being then led by twenty-four beys, who all met at Cairo under a president, called the Sheik-el-Belled. A pasha from the Porte also resided in the country, in order to receive the tribute, but did not directly interfere in the civil administration of the country. This political combination so closely resembles Egypt under the Assyrians, that it is one of the numerous instances in which history, according to the saying, repeated itself.

Under this divided rule of the twenty Egypt remained till B.C. 669 when Esarhaddon fell ill, and Tirhakah endeavored, at the head of an army, to regain possession of the country. In the subsequent year Esarhaddon associated his son Assurbanipal in the government, and retained only the kingdom of Babylon. Tirhakah, in the meanwhile, subdued Upper Egypt, and advanced to Memphis, which he entered in triumph, and drove the vassals of the Assyrian king before him. The news of these events reached Assurbanipal whilst staying at Nineveh, and the Assyrian monarch at once prepared to act, and advanced his army to the frontiers of Egypt. As he proceeded in his march, the countries through which he passed paid homage to the Assyrian ruler; and the ten kings of Cyprus, alarmed at the progress of the Assyrian army, rendered their submission through their envoys to the youthful monarch, who entered Egypt by the usual route of Raphia and Pelusium. In the battle which ensued the Egyptians and Ethiopians were defeated with great loss, and Tirhakah, unable to oppose the advance of the Assyrians, or defend Memphis, embarked on the Nile, and accompanied by numerous fugitives fled to Thebes. The forces of the vassal monarchs of the country then joined the Assyrian forces, and embarking on board another fleet, after forty days' sail on the river, reached Thebes. A second time Tirhakah, conscious of his inability to continue the struggle, crossed the Nile, abandoned Thebes, and finally retreated to Napata or Gebel Barkal. After these great successes Assurbanipal returned to Assyria, having taken the necessary precaution of leaving Assyrian garrisons in the principal cities to secure his conquest. But the Egyptian vassals were tired of their dependency on Egypt, and a league, at the head of which was Necho, was formed, and made overtures to Tirhakah, who seems to have been regarded with greater favor by the Egyptians than the Assyrian monarch. The revolt broke out, but was speedily quelled by the Assyrian generals, who promptly seized the leaders; and Necho, who had been raised to power by Assurbanipal, was sent bound with chains to Nineveh, to expiate the consequences of his unsuccessful attempt to free the country from a foreign conqueror. While these events were in progress Tirhakah had not been idle; entering Egypt he had regained Thebes, and having defeated the Assyrian generals in Upper Egypt, advanced on Memphis. The success of Tirhakah alarmed the Court of Assyria, and Assurbanipal immediately liberated Necho from his chains, and sent

M

him accompanied by an army to again govern Egypt in the interest of Assyria, and to check the progress of Tirhakah. This operation appears to have been successful, for Tirhakah retired at his advance to Upper Egypt, and finally to Napata where he appears to have died. The name of Tirhakah is found on many of the monuments of Egypt; and absolute chronology begins with it, the later years of his reign being linked to that of the twenty-sixth dynasty by the dates of the Apis bulls found in the Serapeum; for an Apis, born in the twenty-sixth year of Tirhakah, died in the twenty-sixth year of Psammetichus I., which proves that the reign of Tirhakah was twenty-six and not eighteen years as given by Manetho, and gives the clue to the chronology of the period. The successor of Tirhakah in Ethiopia was Rutamen, the Urdamani of the Assyrian annals, who was the son of Sabaco, having been displaced in the kingdom of Egypt by his uncle. As soon as he ascended the throne he prepared to wrest Egypt from the Assyrians. In the first instance he appears to have regained Thebes, if indeed he had not held it as an Assyrian vassal. From Thebes he marched upon Memphis, and appears to have defeated the Assyrians and taken Memphis, driving the Assyrians once more from the valley of the Nile. The Assyrian monarch had again to quell the revolt of this important province. The king of Tyre seems to have taken part in the struggle, for Assurbanipal laid siege to Tyre and blockaded it with an investing force. Then he marched to Egypt, passing through Aphek on the frontier of Samaria, and supplied with camels and water by the king of Arabia, crossed the desert which separates the two countries and defeated once more the Ethiopian and Egyptian forces. Rutamen retired in dismay from Memphis, and Assurbanipal after receiving the submission of the Egyptian princes, marched in person to Thebes. Rutamen fled at his approach, the city was taken by storm and plundered, and the palace of Rutamen spoiled. Amongst other objects, the Assyrian monarch removed or threw down two of the great granite obelisks which adorned the temple of Amon. This capture of Thebes is alluded to by the Hebrew prophets.* Once master of Thebes Assurbanipal overran the whole of Egypt, and set up the kings of the nomes, who had been deposed by the Ethiopians, and as Necho does not appear in the list, he had either been killed in the course of the war, or dying, had been succeeded by his son in the government of Sais. The fate of Rutamen and the length of his reign, supposed to be twelve years, are unknown. The Assyrians state that he fled to Kip-kipi. His daughter was married to Pefaabast, a name found in the annals of Piankhi. His successor at Napata or Gebel Barkal seems to have been Nutmiamen, and from a tablet preserved at the site just mentioned, it appears that in the second year of his reign he was induced by a vision to appear once more in the field against the Assyrians, and to attempt the conquest of Egypt. Nutmiamen saw in a dream two uræi ser-

* Nahum iii. 8-10.

pents or cobra di capella snakes, one on the right and the other on the left hand. When he awoke they were not there, and he asked the priests the interpretation of the vision. The explanation of one of the prophets was couched in these words, "Thou possessest the South, thou submittest the North, the diadems of the two regions shine on thy head, thou hast the whole country in its length and breadth." The king proceeded to Napata, entered the temple of Amon, and probably held the sacred image which, according to Diodorus, conferred on him the right of sovereignty. He gave thirty-seven bulls, forty vases of beer and the liquor called *ash*, besides a hundred ostrich feathers to the temple, and his coronation was performed by the priests. From thence he marched and sailed to Elephantine, worshipped the local god Khnum, presenting rich offerings, and went on to Thebes, which he entered apparently without resistance. He was received by Sentur the prophet, and forty horoscopi or astrologers, who offered him the flowers, or crowns of the god. Pursuing his march to Lower Egypt, he was well received by the Egyptians; but he took care to fortify the city of Amon in case of a reverse. "Be received," they exclaimed, "in peace: thou givest life to the double region, thou comest to restore the temple which fell to ruin, to re-establish the gods in their sanctuaries, to make offerings to the departed spirits, and to purify every one in his abode." The connection of the religion of Upper Egypt with that of Ethiopia probably facilitated his march through the

South, but on his arrival at Memphis the state of affairs changed. The kings of Lower Egypt more faithful to Assyria, or unwilling to submit to a Nigritic conqueror, gave battle to his hosts, and received a signal defeat. Pakrur the king of Pasupti, and apparently the chief of the confederation, proffered submission to the conqueror, but as Nutmiamen either then or subsequently fortified Mnu or Hermopolis, it is probable that his success alarmed the Assyrians, and brought them once more into collision with the Ethiopians. At all events, the events of the reigns of Rutamen and Nutmiamen, do not appear in the tombs of the bull Apis in the Serapeum, and must be regarded as comparatively transient in the history of the great struggle for Egypt, at this period too weak to defend itself against its northern or southern neighbors.

The rise of the twenty-sixth dynasty, the last of the native princes which possessed continuous power, sprung from the Saite line of Necho. According to the Greek lists Stephinates and Nechepso* had preceded Necho I. whose fate has been already described in the events of the twenty-fifth dynasty. It would appear from the Assyrian accounts that a son of Necho, probably Psammetichus, had received an Assyrian name; but if this was the fact Psammetichus subsequently resumed his Egyptian appellation. To secure the favour of the Egyptians, Psametik or Psammetichus married the princess Shepenaput, daughter of Piankhi, a king descended in the male line from the unfor-

* Rev. Ant. 1868, vol. xvii. p. 329.

tunate Bokchoris. According to the Greek accounts, the twenty tributaries of kings reduced to twelve in number formed a dodekarchy. Allied by ties of blood and marriage, each reigned peacefully in his

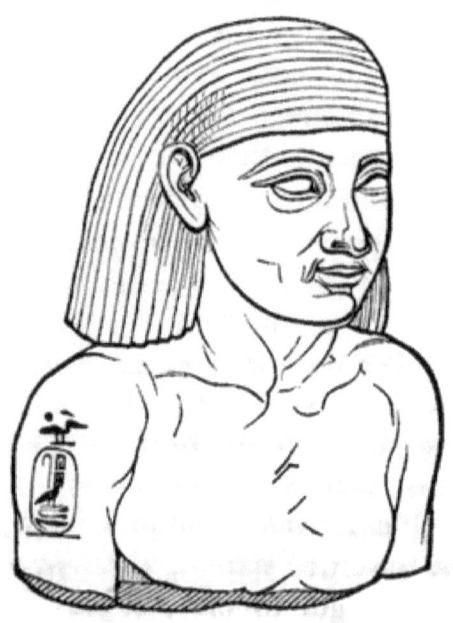

Portrait of Psammetichus. From a Statue.

kingdom, and abstained under treaty from invading the domains of his neighbor. Of all political arrangements such a one is the most provisional, and in the flat and narrow valley of the Nile strategically impossible. It was alone maintained by Assyrian jealousy and armed occupation. The superior wisdom or policy of the house of Sais alarmed the other eleven princes of the dodekarchy, and when Psammetichus had fulfilled, by pouring water out of his brazen helmet, the prediction of an oracle, which asserted that whoever made a libation out of a brass vessel should become sole monarch, the other princes decreed his banishment to one of the most sterile parts of Egypt, but Psammetichus prepared for war. It would appear that the others were under the Assyrian protectorate, and that Psammetichus followed the traditional policy of the Saite dynasty in attempting to recover possession of Egypt. At this conjuncture the Asiatic Greeks rendered useful assistance to Psammetichus. The powerful and wealthy kingdom of Lydia, the head of the Greek confederacy on the western coast of Asia Minor, was ruled by Gyges. Struck with admiration of the power of Assyria, Gyges acknowledged the supremacy of Assyria, and it appears that he received some aid from the valley of the Euphrates in the shape of men, or other means by which he defeated the Cimmerians. But at a later period the disturbed and unsettled state of the Assyrian dependencies caused Gyges to take the part of Psammetichus against the Assyrian power in Egypt, and Gyges sent a contingent of Greeks, principally Carians and Ionians, to aid the Egyptians. An oracle had foretold success to the employment of brazen men who should rise from the sea, and the services of these Greeks in their invulnerable panoplies of brass, turned the scale in favor of Psammetichus, and the Assyrian garrisons left Egypt for ever. The battle, which decided the fate of Egypt, took place at Momemphis the modern Menouf, and Psammetichus rewarded his foreign troops with permanent places of occupation called "The Camps," in the neighborhood of Bubastis. From them arose a class which acted at a later period as dragomans to the Greeks who visited Egypt. The preference accorded by Psammetichus to his foreign troops, who in the Syrian war formed a kind of body-guard, so enraged the Egyptians placed on the left flank, that 200,000 of the national troops are said to have revolted and sought a new country in Ethiopia.

Some of the Greeks left an inscription engraved in the rock at Abusimbel recording that when Psammetichus came to Elephantine those who sailed with Psammetichus, son of Theokles, going beyond Kerkis inscribed it on the rock. This is the earliest Greek inscription to which a positive date can be assigned. Egypt had now lost all her foreign conquests, and her energies were directed to secure her frontiers from invasion. Garrisons at Elephantine, Daphne, and Meroe, protected the Ethiopian, Syrian, and Libyan frontiers. In foreign expeditions Psammetichus appears to have had little success, and the siege or rather blockade of Azotus alone consumed twenty-nine years of his long reign. If, however, Egypt was no longer able to take the field, great attention was paid by the new dynasty to the repairs of the temples and the revival of the arts. At Sais, Memphis, Thebes, and Philæ, the works of Psammatichus I., are found. The great temple of Ptah at Memphis was enlarged, and at the Serapeum of the same place he made a new gallery for the reception of the mummies of the bull Apis, which had died in his reign. The first mummied bull deposited in this gallery died in the fifty-second year of his reign. These bulls were buried with great honor and at a great expense, and appear to have been treated with special veneration, agreeable to the importance assumed by Memphis, once more re-established as the political capital of Egypt. The revival of the arts

Tomb of the Apis of the reign of Psammetichus in the Serapeum at Sakkarah.

at this period is not less remarkable; the principal and favorite material was basalt, especially a green variety. There is great suppleness and vigor in the limbs, but not that vigorous display of anatomical details visible in the older works of painting and sculpture. It was an age of revival, the older works of the fourth dynasty were imitated and copied in all their chief details, with greater smoothness, fineness, and floridity. In literature the older religious works were amended, collated, and arranged in accordance with the canon adopted by the priests. A new form of hand-writing called the *demotic*, or "popular," or else the *enchorial*, or native, came into use and superseded for the ordinary purposes of legal documents and civil life the *hieratic* or sacred cursive or writing hand which had hitherto prevailed. This had probably resulted from the influence of the foreign nations who traded to the ports of the Delta, and had made the Egyptians acquainted with the more compendious Phœnician and the still more perfect alphabet of the Greeks. Egypt was already in its decadence and old age, and the hieroglyphics already represented a dead language, so that a new form of writing was required to express the changes which had taken place not only in the grammatical structure of the vernacular, but also in the body of the language, into which foreign words had already been extensively introduced and which could no longer be adequately expressed by the hieratic. In sculpture the canon of proportion changed, and in architecture the columnar slab, which raised to about four feet, linked column to column, and kept the view of the sacred shrine from the eyes of the profane vulgar, was introduced into the temples. Some of the later shrines were huge monoliths, quarried out of masses of basalt, and their size or beauty excited the admiration of posterity. But in all respects Psammetichus must be considered one of the noblest of the Egyptian monarchs, combining shrewd political knowledge with military talent, and an enlightened love of the arts which decorate and immortalize the present by transmitting to the future a knowledge of the irrevocable past. Necho II., son of Psammetichus and Shepenhap, succeeded to the crown, and he married his sister-in-law Nitakar or Nitocris. The development of the maritime power of the Greeks probably induced him to turn his attention to the marine of Egypt. He conceived the idea of joining the Mediterranean to the Dead Sea, now for the first time realized by the Suez Canal. Necho II. continued the old canal of Necho, which he cleared and enlarged, and his canal starting from Bubastus at the Pelusiac branch of the Nile, entered the Bitter Lakes close to the ancient Pakhetam or Pithom. It must have been of considerable breadth, for two triremes could pass each other as they went along. The work was no doubt executed by forced labor, and 120,000 laborers are said to have perished in the digging. A convenient oracle declared that he was working for the foreigners, and Necho desisted from the too arduous project. With the name of Necho is associated the first recorded attempt of the circumnavigation of Africa. He despatched some Phœnician navigators down the Red Sea with orders to enter the Mediterranean by the Straits of Gibraltar, the pillars of Hercules of the Greeks. In this voyage they succeeded, and proved the truth of their enterprise by bringing back the startling account that they had seen the Sun rise at their left hand. Necho also built dockyards on the shores of the Mediterranean and Red Sea, for the construction of a fleet of triremes, a kind of vessel not used by his predecessors, but with which he had become acquainted through the Greeks. Necho was the last Egyptian monarch who had relations with the Jews. He desired to attack the Assyrians, and marching on Carchemish, was attacked by Josias, king of Judah, who attempted to oppose the march of the Egyptian monarch in the plains of Megiddo. In the battle which ensued Josias, who had disguised himself, was mortally wounded, and leaving his chariot, was carried in another chariot to Jerusalem, where he died. The Jews appointed Joachaz, the son of Josias, as king in the place of his father, but Necho marched on Jerusalem, deposed Joachaz, and condemned the city to a tribute of a talent of gold and a hundred of silver. He then set up Eliakim the brother of Joachaz as king, and took Joachaz with him as prisoner or hostage to Egypt. Eliakim it appears changed his name to Jehoiakim. After the fall of Nineveh to the arms of the Babylonians and Medes, and the extinction of the line of Sennacherib, Necho, probably to secure his Syrian conquests, marched again against the Babylonians, and sustained a severe defeat at Carchemish, where his army was routed by Nebuchadnezzar, son of Nabopalassar, king of Babylon. All Syria, except the country of the Philistines, fell into the power of the Babylonians, whose triumph is celebrated in the prophecies of Jeremiah. Like his father, Psammetichus, the Pharaoh Necho renewed or embellished the different temples of Egypt; and tablets at El Hammamat, which are dated the eighth year of his reign, and those in quarries at Tourah record his care to embellish the monuments of his country. A stelé at the Serapeum mentions the death of an Apis in the sixteenth year of his reign, and that Necho buried the deceased bull with unparalleled magnificence. The other details mentioned on the stelé fix the duration of the reigns of his immediate predecessor and successor. Sais, the seat of the dynasty, shared with Memphis the honors of the capital, and there is every reason to believe that Necho was there buried. The mummy of this king was destroyed about a century and a half ago, the sacred scarabæus placed upon the region of the heart, and inscribed with his name, having been brought to a convent in Paris. Necho reigned sixteen years, and was succeeded by Psammetichus II., son of Necho and the queen Takhauat. His name is found in the island of Elephantine and Konosso, an islet between Elephantine and Philæ, and its presence there is supposed to record a campaign against the Ethiopians, whose kingdom now extended to Syene or Assouan. Psammetichus II. only reigned five years, and was succeeded by his son Uahhapra or Apries, the Hophrah of Scripture. He appears to have vanquished in a naval battle the allied fleets of Cyprus and Phœnicia, and taken Sidon. Laden with the spoils of the Phœnicians, probably at that time the tributaries of the Babylonians, he revived the prestige of the Egyptian arms which had received so severe a shock under Necho II. The Jews, more inclined to the supremacy of Egypt than the domination of Babylonia, revolted for a third time, and their king Zedekiah made an alliance with the Pharaoh, and Apries marched against the Babylonians, who retired at his approach. They returned however to the siege of Jerusalem, which was taken by Nebuchadnezzar, B.C. 558, and Apries appears to have been unable from some unexplained cause either to aid the Jews or raise the siege. A great number of the Jews, and amongst them the prophet Jeremiah, emigrated to Egypt and arriving at Taphnes subsequently distributed themselves throughout Egypt, chiefly in the cities of the Delta. Subsequently Apries made an alliance with Adiacras king of the Libyans, and attacked the Greek settlement of Cyrene, which became menacing to its neighbors. The army of Apries was defeated and the conquered army on its return to Egypt revolted against the monarch, owing to the spread of a rumor that it had been sacrificed to the ambition of Apries. It was in vain that he sent Amasis an Egyptian commander to the disaffected army. The army saluted Amasis as king, and that officer placed himself at the head of the insurgent forces. Alarmed at the conjuncture, Apries sent Patarbemis, another Egyptian, to bring Amasis captive into his presence. The task was too great, for Patarbemis returned unsuccessful to the court. Apries, furious at the want of success, then cut off the ears and nose of Patarbemis, a cruel and ignominious punishment inflicted as already described on traitors. The revolt then became general, and Apries in vain with his army of Greek mercenaries attacked Amasis. Defeated in the battle of Momemphis, he was led captive to his former palace at Sais, and well treated by the conqueror. The nation however clamored for his death, and Apries was strangled and buried at Sais. Such is the Greek history of this later Pharaoh, and his name and titles are found throughout the length and breadth of Egypt. Like his predecessor, he had occupied himself with the erection or embellishment of the public monuments, and had buried with the usual pomp an Apis, which died in the twelfth year of his reign, which lasted nineteen years. His successor Aahmes II., or Amasis, was of an ignoble family and a native of Siouph. It appears he was addicted to the pursuit of pleasure rather than ambition, and his elevation to the throne was more the result of accident than design. His reign continued the policy of his predecessors. At home he embellished the temples of Sais and Memphis, and the numerous inscriptions of the quarries at Tourah, near Memphis, El Hammamat, or the Cosseir Road, and Silsilis, show the extent of his public works. The most remarkable of these was the monolith naos or shrine, brought from Elephantine to Sais. It took 2000 boatmen three years to transport it, and its weight was about 500 tons. An Apis died in the twenty-third year of his reign, B.C. 548, and was buried with great magnificence after seventy days of mourning or preparation. The expense at this period of such rites had increased enormously in proportion with the riches of the country, and the 25,000 towns and villages with which it was studded. The power and importance of the Greeks, now become a kind of janissaries or prætorian guard, encamped in the neighborhood of Memphis, was too strong to be ignored, and Aahmes not only favored the Hellenic population domiciled in Egypt, but opened to the commerce of Greece the port of Naukratis in the Saite nome. The "Guard," as the Ionian and Carian troops were considered, Aahmes quartered at Bubastus in the neighborhood of Memphis, the Northern capital. Either from inclination or policy, the Egyptian monarch particularly cultivated the friendship of Greece and the isles. He offered rich presents to the Delphi, Samos, and Lindos. To the Cyrenians, with whom he had made peace, he sent an image of Athene and his statue, and married Ladike, the daughter of the Cyrenian Kritoboulos. The island of Cyprus, according to Greek accounts, he conquered, but there is reason to think that it had been long prior invaded if not annexed by the Pharaohs, and the arts of the island show unmistakable evidence of Egyptian influence at a remote period. Aahmes married at least three, and apparently four wives during his lifetime. Of these, the most important was Ankhnas, the daughter of Psammetichus II. Her fine sarcophagus of black marble covered with hieroglyphic inscriptions, the prayers of the queen, and the responses of the gods was found at Luxor, and is now in the British Museum. At the close of his reign, Egypt excited the ambition of the rising power of Persia, and Cambyses prepared a military expedition for its conquest. The pretext was the duplicity of Aahmes, who had sent an Egyptian oculist to cure Cambyses of a malady of the eyes. The oculist recommended or lauded the beauty of a daughter of Aahmes, and the Persian ruler demanded her in marriage; but Aahmes, apprehending that his own child would have only the ignoble position of a secondary wife, substituted for her Nitetis, the daughter-in-law of Apries, and the last descendant of the line of Psammetichus I. Indignant at the fraud which had been practised, Cambyses prepared for war, but Aahmes died before the advance of the Persians, and closed, B.C. 527, a long reign of forty-five years, in which he had displayed all the qualities of a good monarch, sagacious statesman, and able commander. His place of sepulchre is unknown, although the satirist Juvenal speaks of his body as torn from the pyramids, probably alluding to the tradition of the vengeance of Cambyses.

The opportune death of Aahmes opened Egypt to the Persians, if indeed it could have been held against the fierce valor of the Persian troops which had already conquered the East and Asia Minor. Phanes, a former soldier of Aahmes and commander of the Greek body-guard of that monarch, had deserted to Cambyses, and led the advance of the Persian army, which traversed Palestine and the Arabian desert. From the Arabian king it received the necessary supply of water carried in jars on the backs of camels, for the Arabian monarch had formerly been engaged in hostilities with Aahmes. Psammetichus offered battle on the Pelusiac branch of the river, and after a terrible conflict, chiefly sustained by the Greek mercenaries on the part of the Egyptians, the Persians gained the victory, and with it the possession of Egypt; for it was in vain that the defeated forces sought refuge in Memphis, and attempted to defend it against the Persians. Cambyses placed in the van of his army the sacred animals of the Egyptians, who, from religious motives were afraid to shoot their arrows at the Persian host lest they should destroy these living idols. The débris of the Egyptian troops covered themselves in the white wall or citadel of Memphis. A Mitylenian galley which ascended the Nile to that city, bearing a Persian herald and a summons to surrender, was attacked, its crew and the herald killed. Cambyses then ordered the assault of Memphis, which was taken after some resistance, and the son of Psammetichus III., and 2000 Egyptians who had been condemned to death were put to the sword. The life of the Egyptian monarch was spared for the time and he was kept in surveillance at the court of Persia, but found to be a useless incumbrance and a dynastic danger; he was accused of conspiracy against Cambyses and condemned to drink the blood of a bull, a mode of execution peculiar to the Persians. He reigned only six months, and his name is scarcely found on the monuments of Egypt. Psammetichus was the last of the independent monarchs of Egypt, as although the Persians were driven out for a time, they conquered Egypt again and reduced the native monarchs to the condition of vassals and the country to a satrapy or administered province, which Egypt ultimately became. The reign of Cambyses over Egypt was not longer than eight years. After the capture of Memphis Cambyses proceeded to Sais, and having exhumed the mummy of Amasis, publicly burnt it, having treated it with the greatest dishonor in his power. Some account of his actions at Sais are narrated in the hieroglyphic inscriptions of the statue of Utaharpenres, a priest and high admiral who lived in this reign. It appears that Cambyses, who conferred an important charge on the officer, assumed a royal prænomen. Cambyses cleared the temple of Neith of the crowd of foreigners who had seized on the precincts, and levelled the constructions they had erected. He was initiated into the mysteries of the temple of the goddess, supposed to be the mother of the Sun, an attractive legend for the fire-worshipping Persians; he then prepared to attack the Carthaginians, the Ammoneum or Oasis of Amon in the desert, and the Ethiopians. His plans were unfortunate, 50,000 men and their general are said to have perished in the sands of the desert while attempting to reach the Oasis. The campaign against Ethiopia was equally unsuccessful, and after some small success on the southern frontier, and great loss of life and much suffering, Cambyses failed in his attempt, and returned maddened to Thebes in the fifth year of his reign, B. C. 525, at the moment of the discovery of a new Apis. Mistaking the public rejoicings for those at his own defeat, he wreaked his vengeance on the magistrates, whom he killed. The priests of Apis were ordered to bring their charge into his presence, and he stabbed the sacred bull in the thigh and bastinadoed the priests. At Memphis he opened the tombs, visited the sanctuary of Ptah, mocked the image of the god and burnt the images of the gods of the circle of Ptah. The town and temple of Sais, according to the legends of the statue already mentioned, were saved "from the very great calamity which happened in the whole country, for never a like took place in this country," by the good offices of Utaharpenres. The revolt of the Magi saved Egypt from further horrors and insult, for Cambyses, whilst mounting his horse at Ecbatana to march to Susa to quell the revolt of the false Smerdis, stabbed himself accidentally in the thigh, according to the Egyptians with the very dagger with which he had wounded the Apis, and at the corresponding place of his own thigh. The name of Cambyses with the date of his sixth year is found on the rocks of El Hammamat. The successor of Cambyses was Darius, called by the Egyptians Tariush or Entariush. Egypt formed part of the African satrapy, and paid a tribute of 700 talents of silver besides the revenues of the Lake Mœris, and 120,000 measures of corn. The civil government of Egypt seems to have been conferred by Darius on Utaharpenres, who

reduced to order the state of the country convulsed by
the madness of Cambyses and the revolt of the Magi.
The administration of Darius was mild; he built or
repaired the temple of Amon in the Oasis of El Khargeh, and worshipped the deities of Egypt; and when
the country was thrown into revolt by the cruelties of
Aryandes. Darius in the fourth year of his reign, B. C.
517, returned to Egypt and offered 100 talents for the
discovery of a new Apis to replace the one which had
just died. Another Apis subsequently died in his reign,
and a third appeared in the thirty-first year of the
same king. Darius attempted to complete the canal of
Necho, and amongst the monuments of his reign at
Suez, may be cited his signet ring, with a representation of Darius in his chariot shooting a lion, and his
name and title in Cuneiform characters in three languages—Persian, Median and Babylonian. Aryandes,
the Persian viceroy of Egypt, was put to death by
Darius on suspicion of treason. He had made an
attack on Cyrene with an army commanded by Amasis
to punish the murderers of Arcesalaus, who had been
assassinated by the natives of Barce; but the Egyptian
army suffered heavily from the Libyans, and the prisoners taken at Barce were transported according to
the Persian custom to another spot in the Empire—to
Bactria, where they founded another town with the
same name. After the battle of Marathon, B. C. 490,
when the Persians were defeated by the Greeks, Egypt
revolted from Darius, and it was not recovered during
the lifetime of the Persian King. His rule had been
mild and his moderation great, so much so that when

he desired to set up an obelisk at Thebes, the priests who had charge of the temple refused the required permission, on the ground that his exploits had not equalled those of the native rulers. In B.C. 485, Xerxes, called by the Egyptians Khshairsha, carried on war with Egypt and reconquered the country, and then prepared for the conquest of Greece. In the interval between Darius and Xerxes, according to an inscription on a tablet later than the Macedonian conquest, Khabash, perhaps a Persian satrap or other foreigner, had ruled Egypt for at least two years. According to the language of the tablet "the god Horus had expelled the evil-doer Xerxes out of his palace, together with his eldest son, letting it be known in the town of Neith to this day." In the second year of Khabash, an Apis had been buried in the Serapeum, and Khabash had fortified the coast against the Persian fleet. Xerxes had, however, compelled the Egyptians to furnish 200 vessels for his great fleet, and they distinguished themselves at the battle of Artemisium. Inscriptions at the Cosseir Road and El Hammamat confirm the fact of the reign of Xerxes having lasted twelve years, as recorded by a Persian named Ataiuhi of the court, son of Artames, a Persian officer who held the same employment in the reign of Artaxerxes the successor of Xerxes. The struggle was now renewed with varied success. The Egyptians called the monarch Inarus, whose name has not been found on any monument, and demanded the assistance of the Athenians, who sent a powerful fleet to aid them, while Artaxerxes dispatched his generals to subdue them at the head of an army of 300,000 men. The Persians, at first victorious, then defeated, were besieged in Memphis, but the Persians raised the siege, destroyed the Athenian fleet and impaled Inarus, the Libyan king, who had fostered the revolt. The Egyptian king Amyrtaios fled to the marshes of the Delta, and the Persians after the six years of struggle placed as vassals or satrap monarchs Thannyras on the Libyan, and Pausiris on the Egyptian throne.

Artaxerxes was succeeded by Xerxes II., who, after a transient reign of a few months, was assassinated by his brother Sogdianus, B. C. 424, who is said to have reigned only seven months. After these domestic revolutions Darius II., the son of Xerxes, ascended the throne and reigned for nineteen years, till B. C. 425. Recent discoveries at El Khargeh or the Oasis have discovered the names and titles of two monarchs named Darius at that spot, and one of them probably belongs to this Darius rather than the monarch of the thirty-first dynasty, whose short reign of four years was too anxious and disastrous, on account of the march of Alexander into Asia, to allow the unfortunate monarch to pay attention to the affairs of Egypt.

The affairs of Egypt from this period are involved in some obscurity, as the authority of the monuments is wanting to confirm or set right the Greek accounts. As, however, the defects of monumental history are at this period filled up by the narratives of foreigners who lived at the period, especially the Athenians, the absence of contemporary monuments is not so important as it otherwise would have been. A second Amyrtaios is the only king of the twenty-eighth or Saite line, and he was succeeded by the twenty-ninth or Mendesian dynasty. The first of its monarchs was Naifaarut or *Nepherites*. He rarely appears on the monuments, although he partly restored the temple of Amon at Karnak; but his name and titles are found on his clay seal in the British Museum, which had been formerly appended to some important state document. Naifaarut reigned only seven years, in the fourth of which he aided the manning and victualling of a Lacedæmonian fleet. His successor, Hakar or Achoris, like his predecessor, combined with the enemies of Persia in the vain hope of more securely establishing his dynasty. Hakar allied himself with Evagoras, the king of Cyprus, who had almost expelled the Persians from that island. The allied fleets were defeated by the Persians, and Hakar after a reign of eight years, left the struggle to his successor. The name of Hakar also occurs on the monuments of Egypt at Alexandria, and Medinat Habu. The thirtieth dynasty, the Sebennyte, was founded by Nekhtherheb, the *Nektanebes* or *Nekhterebes* of the Greeks. This monarch gave the command of his fleet to Chabrias, but that officer was recalled at the remonstrances of the Persian Court. Artaxerxes II. attacked Egypt with an overwhelming force and a fleet of 500 gallies, and a mercenary Greek force of 20,000 men. Nekhtherheb fortified the coast, but the Persian fleet entered the Pelusiac branch of the Nile and disembarked. Dissensions arose between Iphikrates, the Greek, and Pharnabazos, the Persian general; irreparable time and advantages were lost. Nekhtherheb concentrated an army at Mendes, and defeated the Persians, who retired from Egypt. In his reign of nineteen years this monarch renewed the temple of the Delta, especially that of Behbut, and the temple of Khonsu, at Karnak; also that of the god Tum or *Tomos* at Rosetta. The arts had all the elegance, but were more florid than at the period of the twenty-sixth dynasty. Two obelisks of black granite in the British Museum, formerly founded at Cairo, show the admirable finish which prevailed at this period. A beautiful sarcophagus of this monarch is also in the British Museum, and another is known of a person deceased in the fifteenth year of his reign. His successor Getho or Teos, was apparently his son, and his name has been found in the quarries of Mokattam. With an army of Egyptians and Greeks commanded by Agesilaos he held the country, but the Egyptian oppressed the natives by his taxation, and annoyed Agesilaos by his speeches. The army revolted after two years, and Nekhtenebef, the last of the native Pharaohs, was recalled from Phœnicia to mount the throne of Egypt. His right to the throne was disputed by a Mendesian prince, and Nekhtenebef threw himself into one of the great fortified towns of the country, which was invested by the Mendesians, but a successful sortie of Agesilaos defeated the forces on his arrival. The energy of Ochos, the successor of Artaxerxes, however, restored once more the Persian rule in Egypt. Sidon, notwithstanding its Egyptian garrison, was taken, and the Persians, reinforced by Greek mercenaries, commenced the siege of Pelusium. Nekhtenebef, a bad general but jealous of command, directed the operations in person, and alarmed at some Persian successes fled to Memphis which he fortified. The Greek garrisons of Pelusium and Bubastus surrendered, and Nekhtenebef, afraid of offering further resistance, did not even sustain the siege of Memphis, but fled with his treasurer to Ethiopia, B.C. 340, after a reign of nineteen years.

From this period Egypt became a satrapy of Persia, till the conquest of Alexander the Great, B.C. 332; then it became a Greek kingdom under the Ptolemies till the death of Cleopatra, B.C. 30, and finally a Roman province till the Mussulman conquest.

THE END.

An Important Historical Series.

EPOCHS OF HISTORY.

EDITED BY

EDWARD E. MORRIS, M.A.,

Each 1 vol. 16mo. with Outline Maps. Price per volume, in cloth, $1.00.

HISTORIES of countries are rapidly becoming so numerous that it is almost impossible for the most industrious student to keep pace with them. Such works are, of course, still less likely to be mastered by those of limited leisure. It is to meet the wants of this very numerous class of readers that the *Epochs of History* has been projected. The series will comprise a number of compact, handsomely printed manuals, prepared by thoroughly competent hands, each volume complete in itself, and sketching succinctly the most important epochs in the world's history, always making the history of a nation subordinate to this more general idea. No attempt will be made to recount all the events of any given period. The aim will be to bring out in the clearest light the salient incidents and features of each epoch. Special attention will be paid to the literature, manners, state of knowledge, and all those characteristics which exhibit the life of a people as well as the policy of their rulers during any period. To make the text more readily intelligible, outline maps will be given with each volume, and where this arrangement is desirable they will be distributed throughout the text so as to be more easy of reference. A series of works based upon this general plan can not fail to be widely useful in popularizing history as science has lately been popularized. Those who have been discouraged from attempting more ambitious works because of their magnitude, will naturally turn to these *Epochs of History* to get a general knowledge of any period; students may use them to great advantage in refreshing their memories and in keeping the true perspective of events, and in schools they will be of immense service as text books,—a point which shall be kept constantly in view in their preparation.

THE FOLLOWING VOLUMES ARE NOW READY:

THE ERA OF THE PROTESTANT REVOLUTION. By F. SEEBOHM, Author of "The Oxford Reformers—Colet, Erasmus, More," with appendix by Prof. GEO. P. FISHER, of Yale College. Author of "HISTORY OF THE REFORMATION."
The **CRUSADES.** By Rev. G. W. Cox, M.A., Author of the "History of Greece."
The **THIRTY YEARS' WAR, 1618–1648.** By SAMUEL RAWSON GARDINER.
THE HOUSES OF LANCASTER AND YORK; with the CONQUEST and LOSS of FRANCE. By JAMES GAIRDNER of the Public Record Office. *Now ready.*
THE FRENCH REVOLUTION AND FIRST EMPIRE: an Historical Sketch. By WILLIAM O'CONNOR MORRIS, with an appendix by Hon. ANDREW D. WHITE, President of Cornell University.

☞ *Copies sent post-paid, on receipt of price, by the Publishers.*

ANOTHER GREAT HISTORICAL WORK.

The History of Greece,

By Prof. Dr. ERNST CURTIUS.

Translated by ADOLPHUS WILLIAM WARD, M.A., Fellow of St. Peter's College, Cambridge, Prof. of History in Owen's College, Manchester.

Complete in five vols., crown 8vo, at $2.50 per volume.

PRINTED UPON TINTED PAPER, UNIFORM WITH MOMMSEN'S HISTORY OF ROME, AND THE LIBRARY EDITION OF FROUDE'S HISTORY OF ENGLAND.

Curtius' *History of Greece* is similar in plan and purpose to Mommsen's *History of Rome*, with which it deserves to rank in every respect as one of the great masterpieces of historical literature. Avoiding the minute details which overburden other similar works, it groups together in a very picturesque manner all the important events in the history of this kingdom, which has exercised such a wonderful influence upon the world's civilization. The narrative of Prof. Curtius' work is flowing and animated, and the generalizations, although bold, are philosophical and sound.

CRITICAL NOTICES.

"Professor Curtius' eminent scholarship is a sufficent guarantee for the trustworthiness of his history, while the skill with which he groups his facts, and his effective mode of narrating them, combine to render it no less readable than sound. Professor Curtius everywhere maintains the true dignity and impartiality of history, and it is evident his sympathies are on the side of justice, humanity, and progress."—*London Athenæum.*

"We can not express our opinion of Dr. Curtius' book better than by saying that it may be fitly ranked with Theodor Mommsen's great work."—*London Spectator.*

"As an introduction to the study of Grecian history, no previous work is comparable to the present for vivacity and picturesque beauty, while in sound learning and accuracy of statement it is not inferior to the elaborate productions which enrich the literature of the age."—*N. Y. Daily Tribune.*

"The History of Greece is treated by Dr. Curtius so broadly and freely in the spirit of the nineteenth century, that it becomes in his hands one of the worthiest and most instructive branches of study for all who desire something more than a knowledge of isolated facts for their education. This translation ought to become a regular part of the accepted course of reading for young men at college, and for all who are in training for the free political life of our country."—*N. Y. Evening Post.*

Sent post-paid, upon receipt of the price, by the Publishers,

SCRIBNER, ARMSTRONG & CO.,

New York.

EDINBURGH REVIEW.—"The BEST History of the Roman Republic"
LONDON TIMES.—"BY FAR THE BEST History of the Decline and Fall of the Roman Commonwealth."

THE
History of Rome,
FROM THE EARLIEST TIME TO THE PERIOD OF ITS DECLINE.
By Dr. THEODOR MOMMSEN.

Translated, with the author's sanction and additions, by the Rev. W. P. DICKSON, Regius Professor of Biblical Criticism in the University of Glasgow, late Classical Examiner in the University of St. Andrews. With an Introduction by Dr. LEONHARD SCHMITZ.

REPRINTED FROM THE REVISED LONDON EDITION.

Four Volumes crown 8vo.   **Price per Volume, $2.00.**

Dr. MOMMSEN has long been known and appreciated through his researches into the languages, laws, and institutions of Ancient Rome and Italy, as the most thoroughly versed scholar now living in these departments of historical investigation. To a wonderfully exact and exhaustive knowledge of these subjects, he unites great powers of generalization, a vigorous, spirited, and exceedingly graphic style and keen analytical powers, which give this history a degree of interest and a permanent value possessed by no other record of the decline and fall of the Roman Commonwealth. "Dr. Mommsen's work," as Dr. Schmitz remarks in the introduction, "though the production of a man of most profound and extensive learning and knowledge of the world, is not as much designed for the professional scholar as for intelligent readers of all classes who take an interest in the history of by-gone ages, and are inclined there to seek information that may guide them safely through the perplexing mazes of modern history."

CRITICAL NOTICES.

"A work of the very highest merit; its learning is exact and profound; its narrative full of genius and skill; its descriptions of men are admirably vivid. We wish to place on record our opinion that Dr. Mommsen's is by far the best history of the Decline and Fall of the Roman Commonwealth."—*London Times.*

"Since the days of Niebuhr, no work on Roman History has appeared that combines so much to attract, instruct, and charm the reader. Its style—a rare quality in a German author—is vigorous, spirited, and animated. Professor Mommsen's work can stand a comparison with the noblest productions of modern history."—*Dr. Schmitz.*

Sent post-paid, upon receipt of the price, by the Publishers,

SCRIBNER, ARMSTRONG & CO.,
New York.

JUST PUBLISHED.

V.—THE GREVILLE MEMOIRS.
VI.—PERSONAL REMINISCENCES BY THOMAS MOORE AND WILLIAM JERDAN.
VII.—PERSONAL REMINISCENCES BY CORNELIA KNIGHT AND THOMAS RAIKES.

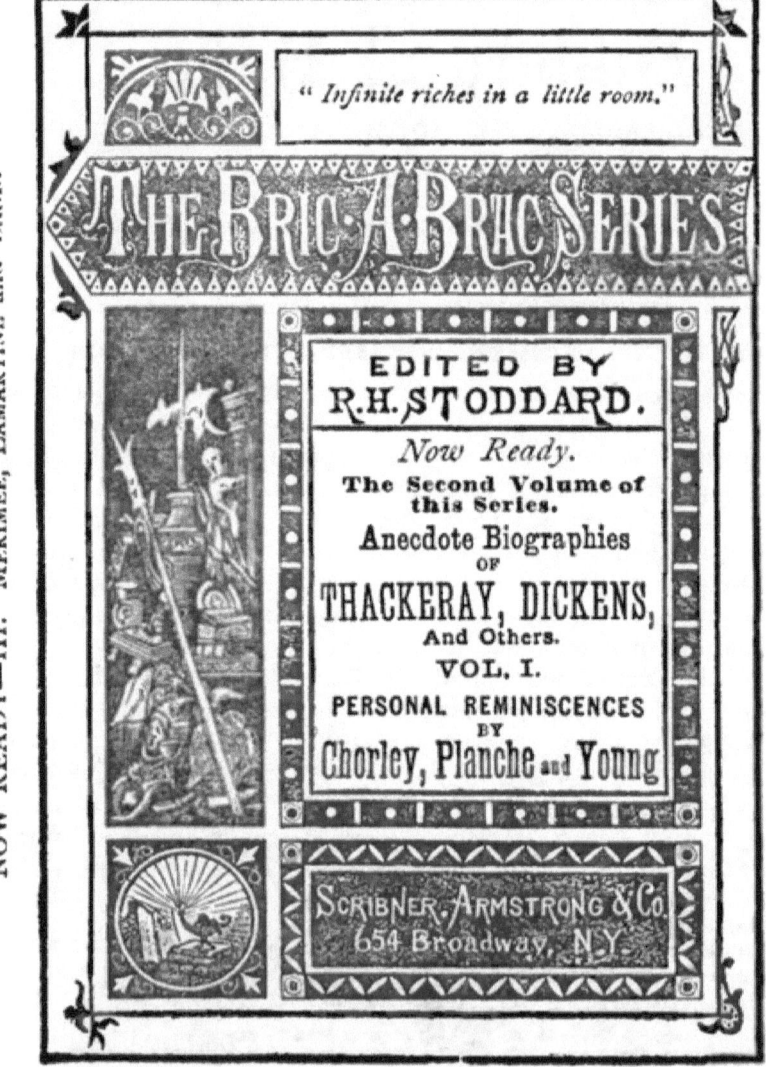

One vol. 12mo, beautifully bound in extra cloth, black and gilt, $1.50.

"No more refreshing volumes could be carried into the country or to the sea-shore, to fill up the niches of time that intervene between the pleasures of the summer holidays."
—*Boston Post.*

"Mr. Stoddard's work appears to be done well nigh perfectly. There is not a dull page in the book."—*N. Y. Evening Post.*

*** SENT POST-PAID, UPON RECEIPT OF PRICE, BY

SCRIBNER, ARMSTRONG & CO., New York.